Campaigning

in Gallipoli

Lieut.-Colonel Cecil Allanson

Edited, with an Introduction by John Wilson

Gosling Press
www.goslingpress.co.uk

Contents

Introduction   Pg I

1   Chapter I En Route   Pg1

2   Chapter II The Voyage To Gallipoli   Pg8

3   Chapter III Joining My Regiment   Pg14

4   Chapter IV The Great Battle For The Chanak Bair Pg21

5   Chapter V The Capture Of Hill 60   Pg36

6   Chapter VI Holding The Line   Pg 48

7   Chapter VII Another Advance   Pg 57

8   Chapter VIII The Blizzard   Pg 65

9   Appendix I   Pg 69

10   Appendix II   Pg 70

11   Appendix III   Pg 73

12   Appendix IV   Pg 73

Introduction

With deadlock on the Western front the allies formulated a plan to attack Turkey, an ally of the Central powers. The theory was if Constantinople was attacked via the Dardanelles it would relieve pressure on Russia and potentially open a supply route to Russia through the Black Sea. It would also potentially take Turkey out of the war altogether.

The original proposal was that this could be achieved purely by naval forces. This concept however failed during February and March 1915 due to the submerged minefield and fortifications along both sides of the strait. With the failure of the naval operation it became clear that if the plan was to continue it would require additional troops to seize the peninsula and destroy the guns and minefields to open the way for the navy to progress to Constantinople. Of course by this time the element of surprise had been lost.

A hastily planned invasion was then put together commanded by General Sir Ian Hamilton. This was a mixed force consisting of British Army forces including the troops from the Royal Naval Division, the French *Corps Expeditionnaire d'Orient*, the 29th Indian Brigade and the Australian and New Zealand Army Corps.

The allied forces landed on 25th April 1915. The initial landings were in some places hotly contested, whilst in others they found only a covering force of Turkish troops. However, the Turks defence proved to be formidable, fighting to defend their homeland rather than the poor troops, which were expected to immediately capitulate.

This led to a stalemate on a par with that of the Western front, which continued until it was finally decided to evacuate the peninsula in late 2015. By the 9th January 1916 the withdrawal was completed, the evacuation was perhaps the best organised phase of the campaign

The published diary of Cecil Allanson is an interesting document not least because of when it was published in August 1916 just seven months after the evacuation. It was a bringing together of the diaries that he kept during the campaign, detailing not only what happened but also his thoughts and observations. Many of these observations are highly critical of the Gallipoli campaign and are more important for the fact that they were not the product of hindsight like many accounts that were published after the war. It is clear that the published diary in some aspects was edited by Allanson and some comments toned down as can be seen when this is compared to his original diary.

Although initially commissioned into the Royal Regiment of Artillery and posted to India and the Madras Garrison Artillery in 1902 he transferred to the 42nd Gurkha Rifles. In 1903 with the reforms of the Indian Army the 42nd Gurkha Rifles was renamed the 6th Gurkha Rifles. Allanson became the adjutant of the 1/6th Battalion. For much of the period between 1908 and 1915 he held a range of appointments including secretary to the Governor-General, Sir Norman Baker and later military secretary to Lord Pentland the Governor of Madras a post he held for three years before being recalled to the 6th Gurkha Rifles for the Dardanelles expedition after Colonel Bruce was wounded

The 6th Gurkha Rifles were part of the 29th Indian Brigade unusual at the time as it had no attached British Battalion. Initially the brigade comprised of the 6th Gurkha Rifles, 14th Sikhs and the 69th and 89th Punjabis. After just over two weeks on the Gallipoli peninsular the Punjabis were withdrawn and later replaced with two additional Gurkha battalions. The 6th Gurkhas performed well during the campaign capturing Gurkha Bluff in May 1915 before Allanson arrived in Gallipoli and taking part in the third battle of Krithia in June. During an attack on the Turkish positions on the 1st of July Colonel Bruce was wounded and evacuated from the peninsular, which precipitated Allanson's recall to the regiment.

Allanson commanded during one of the regiments pivotal actions at Gallipoli. In August as part of a major attack the 29th Indian Brigade, under Major General H Vaughan Cox was to attack Hills Q and 971 located on Sari Bair. This attack started with a night march where many of the troops were delayed or were separated. The aim was to move forward on the night of the 6th August 1915 and capture the objectives by daybreak on the 7th. It wasn't until the 9th August that the 6th Gurkhas assaulted Sari Bair. The Gurkhas succeeded in driving the enemy off the hill and for about 15 minutes occupied the crest, as the 1/6th advanced towards Sari Bair and Maidos from where one can see a large stretch of the Dardanelles, suddenly when they were about 300 feet down, they were shelled. Allanson believed it was the Royal Navy, mistaking them for the enemy, and this has proved a contentious point ever since. By the end of the day the only remaining British officer in the battalion was Captain Phipson, the medical officer as all the other British officers had been killed or wounded. Captain Phipson supported by Subedar Major Pun managed to effect a withdrawal, as the position on Sari Bair was untenable.

In a letter dated August 1916 Allanson commented that there had been some trouble over the printing of his diary as the publication was against the Defence of the Realm act. The printer provided him with three copies and the remaining fifty were to be kept under lock and key until the war ended.

Allanson's spelling in the original diary can be inconsistent and sometimes eccentric (zig-zag in place of zigzag, etc.) this edition retains those inconsistencies

ANZAC & SUVLA

Scale of Miles.

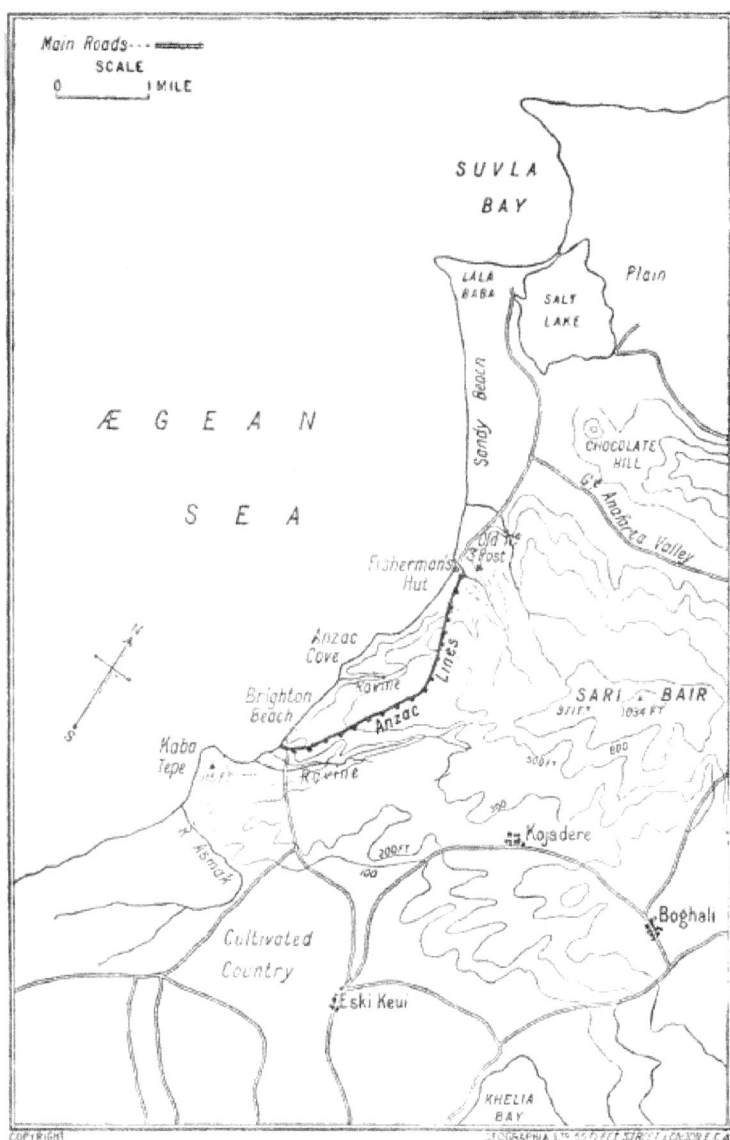

Copy of the Personal Diary

Kept in the field by

Lieut.-Colonel Cecil Allanson

C.I.G. D.S.O. commanding

1ˢᵗ Battalion 6ᵗʰ Gurkha Rifles

20ᵗʰ July to 3ʳᵈ December, 1915

Gallipoli Campaign.

Dedication

This diary is dedicated to the loving memory of those gallant officers, who gave up their lives for their country; during the period I had the honour to command the battalion and whose brave deeds are recorded in it

Captain J. S. DALLAS

6th Gurkha Rifles

(attached) Captain GEOFFREY TOWERS

51st Sikhs (Frontier Force)

Lieut. F. E. Le MARCHAND

56th Punjabi Rifles (Frontier Force)

Lieut. D. I. B. LLOYD

5th Gurkha rifles (Frontier force)

Lieut. H. GREENE

92nd Punjabis

2nd Lieut. H.C. UNDERHILL

Ceylon Planters Corps

The following officers were wounded in these operations:-

Lieut-Colonel C. J. I. ALLANSON

6th Gurkha rifles

Captain A. W. D. CORNISH

6th Gurkha Rifles

(Attached) Lieut. R. L. LEMON

30th Punjabis

Chapter I
En Route

July 1st – Today commences the most eventful period of my life: my orders have come to take command of my regiment in Gallipoli, and I am leaving India immediately. I daresay those around me think I am depressed; it is not depression, it is recognition of the immense trial ahead, the responsibility of other people's lives, and the uncertain knowledge of how my temperament, nerve and physical courage can stand it. Cheerfulness under such conditions is either a wonderful certainty of one's own capacity and self-confidence or a lack of estimation of what active service in the front line against a European enemy means. I am full of thought, my mind is far away, perhaps I appear "distrait" but I know and recognise what the next few months may mean and how everything lies in the hands of fate.

The embarkation arrangements generally in Bombay were not striking, but I successfully got my passage and started off for Port Said in the P&O mail boat "Egypt"

The railway transport arrangements in Egypt are well worked. They have an officer at every important station, and on telling them your duty and showing them the authority they give you the necessary warrant. A subaltern of the 3rd Brahmans met me at Port Said on July 11th, and informed me I was to proceed to Ismailia, and so off I went. The railway transport officer at the latter station advised me to go and see the GOC canal defences, where I am bound to say I met with very little help. I visited our depot which was stationed here, and Captain Hogge, 3rd Brahmans, who was commanding it, did all in his power to assist me. I thought the canal Defence Staff generally looked bored and tired

General Bingley advised me to go on to Cairo to see if the GOC in Egypt, Sir John Maxwell had any orders for me, as none had reached Ismailia. Sir Henry McMahon, the High Commissioner, who has always been very kind to me in India, hearing I was passing through, most kindly asked me to come and see him, and I also received much kindness and help from General Bingley.

There appeared to be about 15,000 troops for the defence of the Canal, a large number of whom are entrenched on the banks. There appears to be no fear of any attack except from stray bodies of Turks. The canal defences are divided up into three sections, each under a brigadier. There seemed to be a good deal of "cross-pulling". Canal defences want things out of India, India wants to stick to its own, Alexandria, the base of the Dardanelles Expeditionary Force, wants officers and men out of the Canal defence force, who are not keen on giving them and so the game goes on.

I stopped at Shepherd's Hotel in Cairo, where everything seemed very gay. Women will congregate where men and excitement are, and one could hardly imagine that we were in a life and death struggle for our existence, and that a few days more would see me among all the horrors of war. Both Sir John Maxwell and Sir Henry McMahon told me that all this loss of life at the Dardanelles was quite unnecessary, and that when the Navy made the first attack, 5000 men could have carried the whole place. They both blamed Winston most awfully.

I could not help thinking of our final scheme at the Staff College, the preparation of a plan of campaign against Turkey, when a lot of the Staff College students decided that the best plan was to create a riot in Egypt bring out a mass of troops from England to quell it, and suddenly shoot them off at right angles to the Dardanelles. This scheme would have worked most perfectly, I imagine instead of the disastrous loss of life that is now taking place.

From Cairo I am sent to Alexandria, where I arrive on July 15th, and proceed to the Majestic Hotel. After much difficulty I discover that the officers of they called the 3rd echelon, to whom I was instructed to report, were at the Hotel Metropole. I went up and saw the AAG, a Colonel O'Leary, who knew nothing about me, not by now an unusual experience! He passed me on to captain Fitzjohn of the Worcester's, who had been blown out of a trench in France in March, and at last after calling up several clerks, a long cipher wire was discovered about me. I was told I ought to return to Ismailia, but that, I said was useless, and what I required was an order enabling me to continue on my journey and get a passage. Fitzjohn said I must go to the Headquarters Base, Mediterranean Expeditionary Force at Mustafa, five miles away and that he would send a letter to that Headquarters about me. I proposed I should take the letter but he said it would go quicker by motor cyclist, and would be there before me, and my orders would then be ready. I wondered and doubted, but thought perhaps Egypt was quicker than India! I drove out in a carriage very slowly to Mustafa, and to find the GOC base when I got there was a pretty big puzzle. At last I laid him low, and was told to go to the garrison adjutant, who sent me to the A.A.G., where I found a rather ancient-looking captain, who said they had never heard of me. I said a message had been sent two hours before by motor cyclist – but as it had not reached them I was told to come again the next day at 12. A ten-mile drive for poor me, to say nothing of the expense! I was told I ought to have gone to Ismailia: I explained I had already been there. They added I might have to wait some time for a passage, as I had not been expected, and there would not be any place on a transport for some time to come.

I believe one good business man would enormously

simplify officers' difficulties: an enquiry bureau with a good telephone service to all the military offices, and a smart fellow in it, would do the business. But I was impressed generally at Ismalia and Alexandria how little the Army works on business lines.

At the Delhi Durbar one would have lost a commission almost for a general arrangement as bad as at Alexandria. A vast army encamped, and never a single notice board, or any help or indication of any kind as to who is who or what is what.

I went out to Mustafa again the next day to see if I could get any orders about myself, and went to the D.A.A.G. Base, Major Ainsworth, R.E. He told me to go to the D.A.Q.M.G., to whom a letter had been dispatched an hour before asking him to arrange a passage for me. The office was next door, but in the hour this distance had not been traversed by the letter. I was told, however, I would not get a passage either today or tomorrow, and that written orders would reach me in due course.

With that I departed, and went over to see my Colonel, Bruce, who was lying in hospital with one very badly broken leg and the other badly damaged. He is a fine optimistic man, with but few complaints; he has been about seven weeks in the Gallipoli Peninsula, and said that from start to finish the whole thing was one long nightmare. Shell, maxim and rifle fire, to say nothing of bombs, without intercession, and that for periods of over a fortnight it had been impossible even to take off one's boots and stockings. He said we suffered from a shortage of machine guns and bombs, the latter being nearly all locally made on the peninsula, and were fighting a very brave enemy, well equipped in a magnificently defended position, and that fear of submarines had greatly reduced the assistance the Navy could give us.

I then on the invitation of the MacMahons, went off to stay with them at their beautiful temporary residence at Ramleh, about five or six miles east of Alexandria. During my stay there they were kindness itself to me, and I am deeply indebted to them. After knowing everyone in Madras it is a pretty lonely business never seeing a soul one knows, and the uncertainty of the future, and the knowledge that it must be a great and immense strain, all tends to make the relief of being with old friends, who probably understand all that is passing in one's mind a truly great one.

Chapter II
The Voyage To Gallipoli

On July 18th I sail in the "Ascania" for Mudros Bay, in Lemnos Island, the base for the operations on the Gallipoli Peninsular.

We had on board the Manchester's (11 Battalion), a divisional cyclist company, and a few other stray people.

I had the opportunity of seeing the type of Kitchener's Army, their officers and their training. The men generally seemed superb, and the officers of this battalion, a regular CO and adjutant and about four officers who had been In the South African War, very good. The colonel gave me to understand they were distinctly above the average. Many of the men looked, and I believe were, blackguards, but they will take a lot of stopping, and I believe the rest of the 10th, 11th and 13th Divisions, all of whom are now moving to the Dardanelles, are just as good. They are a portion of the first army, but he described to me how vast had been the difficulties of training and how much the men had put up with. The result is truly remarkable, and from watching them for several days I should place them up to very near the standard of our best British Indian battalions. Their average age was about thirty. And to think that these men and their officers have been sweating blood whilst our munitions factories have not been organised, and that thousands of good lives are to be thrown away because even now here in the Dardanelles they complain of a shortage of shell. The French have heaps; we have not sufficient.

The fear of submarines is apparent during our journey, and we frequently follow a very zig-zag course. Wounded officers on board the ship returning to their regiments tell one a great tale of how formidable our task is, and how appalling the loss of life as been.

On July 20th the "Ascania" reached Mudros safely, and I am met by a Military Landing Officer, a Captain in the Sherwood Foresters, who started by telling me that the Indian Brigade had recently bolted and let the Turks through. I discovered afterwards, from Major R.E.T. Hogg, Central India Horse, who has flown as an observer or months, that the statement was quite untrue. These wild statements are very damaging, and when untrue only show the difficulty of expecting to have an army when every portion of it crabs the other even to the extent of hopelessly leaving the truth

I had a long and most interesting conversation with Major Hogg, a very old pal. He said when he made his first flying reconnaissance in March there were practically no defences on the peninsular except the forts. Two thousand men with the Navy making a surprise attack could have done the whole thing. Ever since then we have been daily flying over the peninsular seeing them busily preparing the most magnificent defensive position, and the Navy incapable of stopping them. He says someone is terribly to blame, and the Army thinks it is Winston. If Winston was to put his foot near the peninsular I believe he would be scragged alive. He Major Hogg, watched the original landing, and said the seas ran red with blood, and it was the most appalling slaughter he ever saw. The Navy made the whole place quake, but their fire seemed to have very little effect. We have advanced in about four miles now from Cape Helles (no map with me), the extreme western point, but we have fought every inch of our way, and Achi Baba is still untaken. It looks as if it was going to be a very long business and we must have a harbour somewhere well up the peninsular before the rough weather begins in October. Three more divisions have just arrived from home making our force a pretty strong one, I cannot give actual details. Alexandria is the base, Lemnos Island a point on the lines of communication, whilst Imbros Island is where Ian Hamilton's headquarters are. His recent dispatch is not liked. Here they say, and all along the line that too much credit is given to the Chief of Staff. Wherever I have been the pernicious effect of all this distribution of honours is seen. Everyone is nervous in case someone junior or near him should get something and he should appear slighted. Everyone would like to see the firing line rewarded only, but I hear there are a terrible lot of self seekers about, and they tend to eat into the guts of the military administration. Everyone speaks highly of the Turk as a soldier. They say he has not got the vim he had at the start, but that he cannot be despised. The actual conditions at Gallipoli are pretty bad. Flies terrible, mosquitoes bad, heat great, stench appalling, and never any rest from permanent fire. Masses of troops in a crowded space.

Everyone in unanimous that the Indian Brigade has done well, but that depreciates 10 percent for the loss of each British officer, and 20 per cent when the C.O. goes! After our experience in France, this Brigade should have gone up with 30 officers, the same as a British Regiment It would have been interesting to see the result, and an example for all time as to the difference in value. The Indian Officer on whom we rely in peace, and who takes off the BO a vast amount of work, becomes nearly valueless outside India, and his B.O. has all his own work plus all the Indian officers. The Indian Brigade started with two Punjab regiments, the 1/6th Gurkha and the 14th Sikhs. After the first action the first two regiments were relieved by the 1/5th and the 2/10th Gurkhas. It was said to be unsound to use Mohammedan troops against the Turk : we never hesitate in Indian fighting to use Mahommedan verses Mahommedan, Hindu verses Hindu. I know how extremely highly trained the 1/5h and 1/6th Gurkhas are and they have the advantage of six months in Egypt. No troops could be at a higher level of peace training but nothing can compete with eth disastrous effect of the loss of B.O.s. It appears to paralyse a unit completely.

There must be further tremendous casualties before we take the peninsula, and it makes me sick to think of the unnecessary loss of life. Everyone without exception regards it as criminal. One of the greatest crimes in history, and yet I suppose the real culprit will be shielded.

Everyone complains bitterly of want of ammunition, machine guns and bombs. The Turks have cricket ball bombs exceeding ours by twenty yards in range. It is terrible to think that the first three divisions of Kitchener's Army, men of the type that nothing ordinary could stop are coming out with no bombs except what they can manufacture, and only two machine guns (some have three) per battalion. They should have ten. It means their destruction and not giving them a chance. Had we had sufficient bombs and sufficient artillery ammunition Achi Baba might have fallen long ago.

Major Hogg laid great stress on the serious error of sending out no one in real control here who had been to France. Ian Hamilton, Braithwaite, Chief of Staff, the Divisional General and none of his brigadiers, had been there except Simpson Baikie, the gunner General. His experience was of untold use to his arm throughout, and the others would have benefited greatly by more actual personal experience of what modern fighting develops into.

The whole blooming Navy is locked in here and at Imbros, helpless, through these cursed submarines. It is sad to see all those vessels who should be helping the wretched infantry officer in his wearing task, floating at anchor, powerless against three of four submarines which it is known the Germans have here. When an advance takes place on the peninsular, one battleship comes out, absolutely surrounded by torpedo boat destroyers, who dash round and round her, and when she stops to open fire they try to drop nets all around her. In fact, the submarines make the big ship appear valueless. Winston bucked about the "Queen Elizabeth" and showed the Germans the absolute necessity of getting submarines here, and they did it. There is no "Queen Elizabeth" here now! And no more bucking. There seems to be a good bit of jealousy flying about among the higher, and, in fact, all other ranks.

The Headquarters of the Lines of Communication are in the RMS "Aragon" a truly comfortable palace, costing £10,000 a month, I should imagine. It is obvious that it would be infinitely more convenient if they could have been on shore, but I presume there are difficulties to the rapid erection of buildings.

I cannot say one is cheered passing up the Lines of Communication. One cannot but fail to be struck with lack of organisation everywhere, and without it it must be difficult to win a campaign of the magnitude of the one we have undertaken. Few people congratulate one on getting into the firing line. The sights on hospital ships and the tales of wounded men are a proof of the dangers ahead. The bullet, the shrapnel, the bomb, the high explosive, when they catch hold of you, tell their tale, more particularly the last two, whose wounds are truly cruel.

I left the Royal Mail Packet Service "Aragon" on July 23rd, the Headquarters of the Line of Communications, in a trawler for General Headquarters on Imbros Island, ten miles to the North of the peninsula, where I was told the Indian Brigade was in reserve. I certainly gathered from all I saw that we had rushed into this war with Turkey without any real preparation, and with a plan of campaign that would have failed to get a staff college student a p.s.c. There seems a general lack of confidence about, and the wholesale slaughter that has taken place on the peninsula is much resented by everybody and regarded largely as unnecessary.

I had a beastly rough journey, and again failed to stand the elements (Mothersill is I fear, a fraud). My journey was enlivened by the companionship of a nephew-in-law (Mr K. C. Sen) of the Maharaja of Cooch Behar, a postal official. I Left at 11;30am, but as staff work alas! Is so often done, was never informed that I should not reach Imbros till 8 at night, and there was no food of any kind on board

Chapter III
Joining My Regiment

On landing I fortunately saw Cornish of my regiment on shore with a fatigue party, which was very convenient for taking my kit away. General Cox, lately commanding the Rawlalpindi Brigade my G.O.C. was also on the pier, and told me I was to take command of the 6th immediately. I was also very pleased to learn that we had already gained a Brevet Colonelcy for the CO Bruce, 2 D.S.O.s Ryan and Abbott (the latter very badly wounded in getting it) and a Military Cross Poynder. I was also given a good many flattering orders to read, and a hill on the peninsular has been officially given the name of Gurkha Bluff in recognition of its brilliant capture by my regiment. Sad to relate, it cost us the life of one of our finest officers, Captain Birdwood, as splendid a fellow as ever stepped. I found Ismailia had let me down rather badly in telling me I could only take 35lbs of kit, as I found a field officer is entitled to 80 and a C.O. to 160. How much more comfortable I could have made myself, and I do miss a camp bed and chair. I found the regiment in a bivouac and a mess of Captain Cornish, Ryan and Dallas, the latter just returned from Alexandria after a very severe and dangerous wound in the neck, from which most fellows would never have got back, all old officers of the regiment. Captain Phipson, our doctor, had come back to us from civil employment, Lieut Le Marchand, 56th Rifles has arrived as a reinforcement from the Canal, and Lieuts Bear, Underhill and Hearsay are also with us, all planters from Ceylon who have been given commissions and who have done excellent work especially Underhill. I found our mess and general style of living are very much active service conditions without a doubt. Personally I am a very great believer in the British Officer on service making himself as comfortable as he possibly can, and not stinting himself in any way. It may be necessary in a

British regiment but I do not believe in an Indian unit that it is either necessary or advisable. I do not believe being uncomfortable makes the men respect you anymore, and it is all essential that one should not wear oneself out, as the strain of campaign and responsibility is very great indeed. (Nothing throughout the course of the campaign caused me to alter this view; in fact it considerably strengthened it.)

The next day I met all the Gurkha officers and found among them many old friends. A good many of them were drill instructors of mine when I was adjutant. I spent most of the day amongst the men and hope to re-pick up a bit of the language, as I can understand most of what is said. I was amazed to find many of the last draft just in boys of 19, of eight months service. Clearly and obviously the drafts for this regiment should be of the best in the second battalion, old and tried men and not very young soldiers. Why could not all these youths from the depot have been passed to the second battalion, and let us have soldiers of seven to eight years' service? How can the Indian Army be expected to do well when such apparent blunders are made, and troops fighting a really powerful enemy are given boys of eight months service to meet him with Simla, I believe, makes us take men from the depot, and will not let us have men from another battalion, so the adjutant assures me. WE have now a regiment that has done 65 days without a break in the trenches, that has lost half its strength, and to replace it we get fellows who cannot understand a word of Hindustani, little boy recruits. And yet we are shortly to pass out of reserve again. There was very heavy firing indeed last night on the peninsula, gun and rifle fire, and it practically lasted until 4am. The whole day the peninsula was bombarded by our monitors – proof, I am told, and hope truly so, against submarine attack.

I found the whole surplus kit of the regiment in a good deal of muddle. It had been sent over from the peninsula shortly after we got there, and we spent a whole day trying to straighten it out. We have nothing with us but our service kit, now very much the worse for wear, and are renewing it from the kit of casualties. We are supposed to sell these by auction and credit the amount obtained to the estate, but how on earth can this be done on service? And we want the stuff very badly. I fear the men's estate must be allowed to suffer. The whole of our spare kit we propose to leave here, and have neatly parked it away and marked it so that each man can easily recognise his own.

We have attended some lectures on the use of poisonous gases which we are assured will be used against us, and most of the men and officers are inoculated against cholera.

It is very essential to get the men well together again, and with this object we do close order drill for three hours a day, which is excellent for discipline, and gives both men and officers an opportunity of getting to know each other like nothing else. From everything I have heard it is quite evident that immediately heavy casualties occur among the British officers there is a very good chance of demoralisation setting in among the men who have to meet a brave and good enemy, who certainly is brave and reckless with his own life. Every Friday we do a night march to keep accustomed to that class of work; on Saturday morning nothing, and in the afternoon a run across the hills. Specialists are daily at their job, and in the three weeks it was really wonderful to see how smart the battalion was. They caused quite a lot of admiration among the new Army who were busy landing and bivouacking, waiting for the grand advance.

The Indian does not fight for any Government or for any principle, though theoretically it is said that he does. He fights through discipline and the genuine love of his own officers, whom he has been brought up to revere and respect. The fact that he has a reputation, I believe, he only learns through his

British Officer, and I do not really think he personally cares very much about that, though his British officer does most intensely, and has caused that feeling to spread through the ranks.

I am afraid the firing line and the regimental officer have no love for the staff of the higher formations. Nowadays these live in such comparative comfort and so much out of danger; they have the whip hand over one, and very much the ear of the G.O.C. ; they cannot extend their sympathy to those too much who have to go through discomfort, hardship and daily and nightly risk their lives; they should try and let them see and understand that they knew this, and yet if the percentage of rewards given on the peninsula including all those officers and men who left it wounded and sick, was worked out compared to those received by the staff, the result would amaze the world. (a very large number of "legions of honour" were given to the Gallipoli force, and yet despite the enormous losses that we had both in officers and men, through six months hard campaigning, not a single one reached an officer or man of the brigade, and yet all the personal staff of the Commander-in-Chief each received one; comment is needless.) This is a regimental officer's war; there is no grande tactique; every yard that is won is taken through the initiative and capacity of the regimental officer and retained through his bravery and those of his men. It is not easy to picture their feelings when cowering in their trench under our bombardment, the officer, with his watch in hand, knowing that at a fixed hour he must leap from his trench and dash forward to what is almost certain death or serious wound, and if unsuccessful he will be left between the lines to slowly die. If successful he has to dig like hell and be ready for the inevitable counter-attack. Or picture the other side, the men crouching in their trenches with shells of every size and description bursting all around them and knowing that suddenly the range will lift 100 yards to prevent reinforcements coming up, and row after row of Turks will hurl themselves at the trenches.

I fear there is no more chance of my getting any more officers. I have 650 men, of whom about 300 are war-worn worriers. 200 men have just arrived in a draft, about 60 of them very young recruits of six months service. The remainder men from the 2/6th, and certainly not their best, and the remaining 150 men have returned from being wounded, some slightly, some severely and some already for their second time. It would of course be much better if all except slightly wounded men could be allowed to return to India and let us have fresh men, but of course there are disadvantages to this course, as India might be much affected by so large a body of wounded men constantly returning, and a wounded man if his nerve has not gone is full of experience. From comments in the lines it is obvious that men do feel being sent back time after time it naturally gives them a sort of despairing feeling that they have little hope of escape.

All troops were paraded today, July 30th, to hear a message sent from Lord Kitchener to say that there had been another great victory in Mesopotamia, and that the road to Baghdad was now open. With the force at their disposal I cannot imagine how they can ever hope to get there, and if they do how they hope to be able to hold and keep such a vast city. We have naturally made as much of this to our men as we can, but it looks as if the Turks have wisely withdrawn troops from there to add an Amy Corps to what we have meet shortly: not a very inspiring thought, and will make an already overwhelming task more difficult.

When I want to know when this war is over is (1) Had the War Office any plan of campaign ready prepared? (2) |What it was; and (3) How much of it has been carried out on this occasion?

It is quite evident that we are going to make another landing somewhere, as not only have about twenty monitors arrived, but all the battalions are busy practising landings from special boats which appear to have come from home. They are a sort of bullet proof barge, holding closely packed about 500 men, worked by a motor engine, and have a very rapid method of exit, for as they hit the shore the front falls forward and makes a kind of pier.

Hey say this place smells of spies, and so the Turks are probably much interested in what we are doing. It is difficult to find out what is going to happen, but it is interesting to note that the bakery have orders not to cook any more bread after the 5th August, which would look as if this was our date of advance (such it proved to be). It is funny how immensely difficult it is to keep a military secret, and here is a department possibly solely imbued with the idea of economy which may be giving away the whole show.

However the future will prove whether the Turk is ready for us or not, and I only hope we may be able to get a bit out of him this time. With the memory of the 29th Division in one's mind and in that of everybody else's, one cannot expect to feel over cheery about the whole matter until at any rate we are on the move

I have seen a good deal of H.M.S. "Talbot" now in Imbros harbour (Captain Trimmer R.N.); they have frequently in the earlier stages of the campaign given us the most invaluable support and have often sent off their pinnace and doctor to help our wounded after nightfall.

Everybody talks freely about our fresh advance, and as we have been told that we must be prepared to move without transport and to travel light, and later to be able to pick up the rest of our stuff from here it looks as if it must be Suvla Bay.

On August 1st I was ordered to leave the regiment, and to proceed with other C.O.s to an unknown destination and to prepare plans for the great advance.

Chapter IV
The Great Battle For The Chanak Bair

2nd August – I crossed over to Anzac from Imbros with the Brigade Commander and battalion commanders of the Indian Brigade, and saw for the first time the perfectly magnificent – in fact awe-inspiring position that the Australians succeeded in capturing when they landed on this peninsula. I can only describe it as looking through glasses at the Simla Bazar as one comes up the opposite side of the valley in the train : it is simply a multitude of people living in the most extraordinary dug-outs in the side of a steep cliff, height about 350 to 400 feet. I can describe it better perhaps when I give the account of my own regiment's short sojourn in this place.

A most unpleasant landing. The ship is suddenly under shrapnel and two of our small party in the vessel, an Australian officer who was talking to me at the time (Wilson) and a naval landing officer, I think are both hit. I had to pay a good many visits to this the only pier, whilst I was in Anzac, and I never failed to come under shell fire or see very many casualties. It seems a remarkably poor way of ending one's life, without even seeing your enemy. I do not know why the pier could not have been widened and a big centre bullet proof wall of boxes erected: this would at any rate have prevented half the casualties. The pier is surrounded by sunken pinnances, and pier duty cannot be a very charming job.

We were escorted up to general Birdwood's headquarters, where we met Skeen (Brigadier-General, General Staff) Wagstaff G.S.O. 2 and several other officers. Our kit was taken over to the dug-outs allotted to us and we were sent out on a torpedo-boat destroyer to reconnoitre the country over which we were to act: I cannot recommend a more satisfactory way, as I think you get views in your head which you cannot eliminate when you actually get on the ground itself. We wandered up and down the coast for four hours, and the Chanak Bair ridge, which is the key of the whole peninsula, was very plainly shown us: when the method of attack was disclosed to me confidentially that afternoon I gasped. It is to be remembered that Anzac is completely invested by the enemy, that no one has been able to reconnoitre the ground outside, and that no one can absolutely guarantee the map. There are no villages and no inhabitants to help one, and the whole country seemed to be stiff, with very sharp rocky cliffs, covered with thick scrub (and such it proved to be).

I have a few ideas about night marches, and their great difficulty, and the need of careful reconnaissance, but when I was told that we were to break through the opposing outpost line at 10pm on the 6th, march along the sea cost for three miles then turn at right angles and attempt to get under this big ridge about two miles inland, by dawn, and covered from the sea by innumerable small hills and nullahs, I felt what one would have done to a subaltern at a promotion examination who made such a proposition. The more the plan was detailed as the time got nearer the less I liked it, especially as in my own regiment there were four officers out of seven who had never done a night march in their lives. The one hope was that the scheme was so bold it might be successful. My regiment was still at Imbros, ten miles away, and it was decided to bring them over only the night before the great advance in trawlers so as to ensure as much surprise as possible. Two divisions were to be landed from Imbros at Suvla Bay besides others from Mudros and Mitylene, and the whole of the troops on the peninsula already were to co-operate by movements forward.

The four or five days which this portion of my diary covers were spent in the necessary preparations for the carrying out of this plan: the more I saw of it the less I liked it, but I did not tell that to another soul. On the 5th I got leave to bring over our Gurkha scouts to have a look at the position from the torpedo-boat. It is gratifying to learn that everybody admires and speaks well of the Gurkha.

I got disastrous news whilst at Anzac. Ryan my Adjutant has gone sick with dysentery, a simply splendid officer and an untold temporary loss to the battalion. Lieut. Bear has just sprained his ankle. I have now to go into the teeth of the Turkish Army with Captain Cornish, who has already had a pretty rough time of it at Helles, Captain Dallas, full of grit, but has just returned from a very severe wound in the neck, which would have killed most people, Lieut. Le Marchand, 2nd Lieut. Underhill, and that is all. No quartermaster, no signalling officer, no machine gun officer, and yet throughout all their operations these services were maintained and very well maintained to all credit to those trained so fine a battalion for splendid efficiency of the result.

I made a good many reconnaissance's by field glasses only from the highest point of Anzac, but they were mighty unsatisfactory. I also made the Gurkha scouts do the same.

4th August – A year ago war was declared, and today I start the biggest operation of my life: I prayed for courage and the nerve to get through if I could live, which I frankly did not anticipate. The anticipation of such a trial has to be borne to be understood, the responsibility for the lives under one, many of whom one can never hope to see again. A mistake may cost one dear. I have written a few farewell letters; those who get them will have some small idea of what I am passing through. This diary may never be completed: one is up against it for the first time in one's life: the fortune of war holds the scales.

5th August – at 9.30 pm tonight my regiment comes over,

and today the Australians are crowding up to make room for us. Little rabbit holes in a steep cliff is all we have to get in 600 men: sleep will be impossible, I should imagine throughout tomorrow.

I have been several time over the Anzac defences: the landing there on April 25th was an apparent mistake, and was meant to be at Gaba Tepe, but the strong tide overcarried the ships, and extremely lucky it was that they did, as had the landing been there, as the Turks apparently knew it was to be, not a man would have got ashore. The Anzac cliffs seemed so inaccessible that no one would believe they ever could be assailed, and the enemy had not defended the beach at all. The Australians landed, rushed the cliffs, and dashed on despite orders (they are magnificent troops, but their lack discipline is a weakness), and about 2,000 of them were never heard of again. They consolidated their position and absolutely dug themselves in: in many caves their communication trenches are tunnels, and the whole is beautifully clean and well kept. Thos. Cook ought to buy the whole site and make it into a resort for globetrotters: as a wonderful bit of work which sort of put itself together, it is remarkable. All this time we were daily shelled, and were beastly uncomfortable.

At 9:30pm I went down to the pier to find that although my regiment had arrived outside they would not be able to land till about 4.30 am on the 6th which means that the night before the great ordeal my poor little fellows will not get a night in bed. Bad staff work and very hard luck on regiments, many of whom suffered the same fate. At 4.30 am (6th) they rolled up; many had been sea sick, and as best as I could I fitted them into dug-outs: terribly crowded, frightfully hot, and we were shelled all day, losing over 20 men. Then a shell burst the fresh water tank, and I could not get water to cook two days rations till very late, and had great difficulty in getting my men's water bottles filled. I was told this must do for 48 hours, perhaps longer, and the temperature by day is near 100 degrees: further there would be no hope of any more rations or sleep during that period. It turned out to be 96 hours not 48. I went round all the men and impressed upon them the immense necessity of husbanding food, water and ammunition: they are loveable little fellows, and were quite bright and cheery, but one's heart could not help bleeding for what I knew they must go through.

The orders were to break out at 10.30pm, an Australian brigade leading, then the 5th, the 10th, and the 6th Gurkhas, New Zealand sappers, an Indian Mountain battery, the 14th Sikhs. It was a very slow business getting out of our dug-outs in single file, but the regiment was awfully good, and the officers reformed them all on the beach, companies and sections complete. Unfortunately the regiments in front never waited for us, not giving one time to collect the men, and I had to go off on my own: after half an hour of deadly funk as to where I was, I ran into the rest of the column halted. It was now 12.15 midnight, and we were two hours behind our programme time. There was a feeling of panic and doubt in the air as to where we were and where we were going: it was a pitch black night. Suddenly I heard a rush in front; I thought it was the Turks and drew my revolver, and was almost at the same moment knocked down: Dallas behind me fixed bayonets and stopped the rush; it was only a panic of a few men in the regiment in front. Later an order was passed down to turn about and go back : I refused to take it and went up the line to find whose order it was: the C.O. in front had not had it or given it and I found it originated from a hospital assistant, who will I hope be suitably dealt with. Later down came an order to extend to the right, which was again a false one, I discovered by the same method. By this time I knew the state of everyone's nerves.

We were supposed to be at the foot of the hills two miles inland by dawn, but were still on the edge of the sea.

Apparently the Australian infantry brigade in front had very successfully got us out, as we came across no wire and no enemy, and were well out of Anzac. As dawn broke, I saw a column about three miles in length in fours under a low series of hills on our right; a replica of Magersfontein – a burst of fire and I felt we were done. I dashed up a few Gurkhas and a body of Turks immediately threw p their hands, and we took them prisoners; the rest of their trenches were empty. The Turks were apparently more frightened than we were; they must been bad! There was no hope of making an attack by dawn on the Chanak Bair hill, but the Australians were sent off to the left flank to advance whilst I was to support them; the other regiments went off up the right (southern) branch of Aghyl Dere. The place was covered with dead and dying many in great pain, and throwing themselves about: one begins to know again what war was.

I followed up the Australians, and found them hopelessly stopped by a big precipice in front, and so I swung on to the lower ground to the right and let the G.O.C. (Cox) know that the best support I thought I could give was to make a frontal attack, making full use of the hilly country. On my way I found quite a big Turkish camp deserted with lots of rifles, ammunitions, bombs, horses, tents etc. which made me feel very hopeful; we had had great luck. The great thing now was to push on everyone at all costs; alas! It was not done.

I pressed on and got over half way up the hill with practically no resistance when I got a message to go no further forward, but to take up a covering position for the night to protect other regiments now being pushed on behind us. Far better have let me go on, as the later operations proved. A most tiring day: we took up a good position on three hills, which we entrenched well. Had our movements only been more rapid we might have had a brilliant success. The regiment was splendid throughout the day, the 7th. I kept one double company in reserve and put three in the outpost line under Le Marchand, Dallas and Underhill. They had to be much on the alert all night, our third with little sleep.

8th August – Unfortunately the operation orders for the attack next day on the hill at dawn did not reach me until 1.30 am, and I had to get them all out to the outpost line. We had been heavily shelled that evening, and I had been much frightened: we had no blankets and no coats, and when I got the orders I was so shivering with cold (fright!) that I could with difficulty read them. My regiment was ordered to make a frontal attack, leaving at 2.45 a.m., supported by two British battalions, and I arranged to send the outposts direct to the position of assembly allotted. The officer who issued the orders had never seen the country, he had never had had a chance and the point of assembly was the junction of two nullahs, each two feet wide. The confusion was of course, awful, and as I could not get into touch with either the North Staffordshire or South Lancashire, and to get on was all important, I started off to the attack on my own, asking other regiments by note to follow. We were then two and a half hours behind the scheduled time for the attack. The ground was covered with horrible scrub, was all nullahs two feet deep with very steep sides. I advanced in more or less open formation of company columns, and got forward to within 500 yards of the objective (hill 971) without any trouble at all: this I decreased by 200 yards by short rushes. I recognised that reconnaissance and knowledge of the position was so important that I decided to be with the firing line in front and left the adjutant to control behind. Dallas and Underhill both came up, each with about 15 men, but all the rest of their double companies were close: they were working slowly up picking their way splendidly. Suddenly Dallas went down, hit through the head; shortly after Underhill fell, and I saw reinforcement was essential. I went down to find the nullahs all full of men, but the moment a man got out down he went, and this did not encourage others: the regiments should have moved up in open formation. I got hold of an officer (Radcliffe), North Staffords, and two subalterns, and said I must get more men up, we managed to push 50 or 60 on: we got the regiment and these men another 50 yards on, when casualties, including both subalterns, stopped us. I went back again o try and get some more men, and got two officers and 50 Warwicks, and again we got another 50 yards. I then got forward right under the final crest with le Marchand, about 10 Gurkhas and 30 Britishers, with all the rest of the regiment just below.

Further movement was impossible: I was now 9.30 a.m. and blazing hot; I lay there without moving till 6p.m. with every conceivable shot flying in the air about one, shrapnel, our own maxims, rifles and our own high explosives bursting extremely close, which told me how near we were to the top. I lay between two British soldiers; the man on my left had a Bible and read it the whole day; the man on my right I found was a corpse. I wondered if I ought to make good resolutions for the future, and did not. The sun on one's back was most trying.

Immediately it got dark I got all the men up another 50 yards, and then we dug in like hell. Le Marchand joined me with all the men he had left – he had been superb throughout the day: we got quite a good line, but above u, at an angle of about 35 degrees, and only 100 yards away, were the Turks. I sent a message down to G.O.C. and told him how precarious my position was, and asked for pistol flares, but there were none available. I was terribly afraid of a bomb attack, as they had only to roll them down the hill. I still had Cornish, who had been very good throughout, Le Marchand, the bravest and most perfect fellow on service one could ever wish to have: Dallas and Underhill I have lost. Dallas, I subsequently found had gone off to a hospital ship very seriously damaged in the forehead, and it is improbable that he will recover; a most gallant officer, an old friend of mine or whom I have the deepest regard and admiration, who has done me proud: an unselfish comrade, an exceptional character for a man! Poor Underhill, a novice at soldiering but gallant and dauntless. He was a planter in Ceylon before the war, and rose from the ranks of the Ceylon Planters' Corps to a commission with us: he had put in splendid work as quartermaster, was most untiring, obliging and hard working.

Night of 8th–9th August – I went down to the battalions nearest me, the Warwick's, South Lancashire's and North Stafford's, and asked them to give me what support they could as I said I said I did not want to lose my line, and I had put every man in the firing line, as they knew how to deal with a bomb attack: all I wanted was a reserve, They all said "What orders have you?" I explained that my G.O.C. was 3000 yards away and 1000 feet down, and could not in the least realise what was going on, and it was for us to act. The South Lancashire's gave me two companies and the Warwick's one; the entire three regiments should in my opinion have pushed up an joined me. I got telephones out along the line, scraped a little hole for myself and prepared for another sleepless night. During the night a message came to me from the G.O.C. to try and get up on to 971 at 5.15am, and that from 4.45 to 5.15 the navy would bombard the top. I was to get all troops near me to co-operate. Baldwin's brigade would come up on my right, it was hoped, for certain.

By this time the enemy had discovered I was immediately below them, and throughout the night there was a perfectly terrific fire; my wee dug-out was a mass of dust flying about; Phipson our doctor slept beside me, and Cornish next with the telephone glued to his ear. The men fired over 120 rounds on average each throughout the night. The roar was incessant. I was rather weak from want of food and I trembled most of the night. The Navy greatly helped us by keeping their searchlight on the hill, which enabled my fellows to keep the Turks from getting up to rush us. At 4.30

a.m. (9th) I telephoned to Le Marchand my plans for the attack, which I had not told him before as I felt it might be stopped, and I did not want a disaster. He telephoned back "Right Major everything is quite clear" and we compared watches. As I could only get three companies of British troops, I had to be satisfied with this. All the Company Commanders regarded the plan as hopeless, and the cliff to steep to get up, and asked if my regiment would lead. I said "No we must all go up together, in one line; it makes our strength appear greater, and the attack must take place at all costs," and that those were my orders.

I had only fifteen minutes left: the roar of the artillery preparation was enormous: the hill was almost leaping underneath one. I recognised that if we flew up the hill the moment it stopped we ought to get to the top. I put the three companies into the trenches among my men, and said that the moment they saw me go forward carrying a red flag everyone was to start. I had my watch out, 5.15 I never saw such artillery preparation; the trenches were being torn to pieces: the accuracy was marvellous, as they were only just below. 5.18 I had not stopped, and I wondered if my watch was wrong. 5.20 silence: I waited three more minutes to be certain great as the risk was. Then off we dashed all hand in hand, a most perfect advance and a wonderful sight. I did not know at the time that the G.O.C division Godley was on a torpedo-boat destroyer, and every telescope was on us. I left Cornish with 50 men to hold the line in case we were pushed back and to watch me if I signalled for reinforcements. At the top we met the Turks. Le Marchand was down a bayonet through the heart. I got one through the leg, and then for about ten minutes we fought hand to hand, we bit, fisted and used rifles and pistols as clubs; blood lying about like spray from a hairwash bottle. And then the Turks turned and fled, and I felt a very proud man: the key of the whole peninsula was ours, and our losses had not been so very great for such a result. Below I saw the Straits, motors and wheeled transport on the roads leading to Achi Baba.

As I looked round I saw we were not being supported and thought I could help best by going after those who had retreated in front of us. We dashed down towards Maidos but had only got about 300 feet down when I saw a flash in the bay, and suddenly our own Navy put six 12-in monitor shells into us, and all was terrible confusion: it was a deplorable disaster; we were obviously mistaken for Turks, and we had to get back. It was an appalling sight: the first hit a Gurkha in the face; the place was a mass of blood and limbs and scream, and we all flew back to the summit and to our old position just below. I remained on the crest with about 15 men; it was a wonderful view; below were the Straits, reinforcements coming over from the Asia Minor side, motor cars flying, we commanded Kila Bahr, and the rear of Achi Baba and the communication to all their army there. A message came up to say Cornish had been badly hit, and had gone, and I was now left alone much crippled by the pain of my wound, which was now stiffening and loss of blood I saw the advance at Suvla bay had failed, though I could not detect more than one or two thousand Turks against them, but I saw large reinforcement being pushed in that direction. My telephone lines were smashed, I could not leave the regiment, and doubt if I could and have got back.

Victory was slipping from our grasp and all in my neighbourhood, from want of dash, and at Suvla from want of appreciation of how little there was in front of them. Poor le Marchand! For 96 hours he had not slept, and he died a magnificent death, a superb fellow, and he served me truly well. I hardly knew him, and he did not belong to us but to the 56th Rifles Brave as a lion, he worked till he died. I now dropped down into the trenches of the night before, and after getting y wound bound up proceeded to try and find where all the regiment was; I got them all back in due course, and awaited support before moving uphill again. Alas: it was never to come, and we were told to hold our position throughout the night of the 9th–10th

During the afternoon we were counter-attacked by large bodes of Turks five times between 5 and 7 p.m., but they never got to within 15 yards of our line. Our three maxims had got up. All honour to the men who had got that load and all the ammunition up 1,000 feet; the ground in front of us was strewn with corpses in heaps, like the sheave on a harvest field. Every man remained glued to his trenches, with their rifles almost red hot: how I admired them and how I blessed them. It all wanted courage, after four nights without sleep, only two days meagre rations, and one water bottle. Late that evening I was ordered down, and Captain Tomes, 53rd Sikhs, a fine soldier, came to take my place. I told him to be careful, as it was a most unhealthy spot; early the next morning poor fellow he was shot through the heart, and with Le Marchand is buried on the highest summit of Chanak Bair, all honour to them both. It was well I was ordered back to make a report. I was very weak and faint, and should have collapsed during the night. There is nothing like pain to weaken one, and I had to be helped down. The nullahs on the journey back were too horrible, full of dead and dying, Maoris, Australians, Sikhs, Gurkhas, and British soldiers, blood and bloody clothes and the smell of dead now some two days old. I gave morphia(I always carry it) to every so many men on my way down who could get no further and were obviously done.

On arriving down I reported to the General, looking like nothing on earth, my clothes and accoutrements in ribbons, filthy dirty, and a mass of blood. I told him that unless strong reinforcements were pushed up, and food and water could be sent us we must come back, but that if we did we gave up the key of the Gallipoli Peninsula. The General then told me that nearly every-where else the attack had failed and the regiment would be withdrawn to the lower hills early next morning. At 7pm a message came from the Divisional General, Sir A.

Godley, to say he wished to know the name of the regiment and C.O. who had conducted the frontal attack on Hill 971. My regiment's name and my own were sent to him, and a telephone reply came to say that I was to be told that he was proud to have a regiment that had done so well in his command, and that he had watched it all from the sea. (I fancy a good deal of flattery is flung about, but the regiment did deserve the remark.) General Cox then told me officially in front of his staff, just as I was going to hospital that he was recommending me for a V.C. and would have Le Marchand too, had he lived. I can certainly say that it was not a V.C. attack; I only obeyed orders throughout, and could not have done otherwise: it was a theatrical feat, and I think it would have been fitting to have given the regiment a V.C. and let them choose who should wear it. The thanks is due to a splendidly trained regiment, for which I was in no way responsible. Dallas, Underhill, Le Marchand and Cornish all did more than I did and all have suffered infinitely more than myself. I was lucky through these four days. I lost three orderlies, all one after another, but except for my wound and a bullet which just missed my ankle, I had nothing so very close to me as to be a complete nerve shaterer.

10th August – I am now in the Field Ambulance: I hope shortly to be back with the regiment with luck; the bayonet went in about 5in, the sciatic nerve is damaged, and I do not feel much power in the leg blow the knee, but I am alone left, and cannot, unless it gets very serious, leave the peninsula. Our loses were 100 per cent of the British Officers, 60 percent of the Gurkha officers, and 52 percent of the men. I am lying on the ground in a tiny little dug-out, with no comforts but the ordinary daily ration, and am now writing this diary and my regimental despatch.

It may be of interest to note a few of the impressions left upon me in one of the greatest soldier battles ever fought, and the greatest I can ever hope to take an active part in. (I do not mean to infer I ever want to again, because I do not.)

The Turks repeatedly had an aeroplane over us, and learnt a lot from it, that was clear. We seemed, to me, to have only one, and should have had up several to prevent them gleaning information.

The new Army had been trained for trench warfare; we fought as on manoeuvres in India; we had few trenches against us and not much artillery once we got well under the hill, only a few maxims and no wire: their rifle fire was the devil. With the number of troops available everyone determined to get home, and less tendency to constantly reorganise instead of pushing on, we should have won. There could be no previous reconnaissance; no one quite knew were the position was, and troops were undeniably tired after two nights without sleep and terribly short of water. When troops get safe into nullahs it is the devil to get them out. Had we advanced up the hill in lines of battalions in double company columns we should have got home. It was a case, I think of every C.O. with the firing line, so that he could make as much reconnaissance as possible for the future, and every influence was wanted to get on forward and up. We dress exactly like our men and do not wear badges of rank. The latter point is ridiculous. What enemy can see a badge of rank, and it is invaluable to let your own people, and as appears to happen often, troops near you know who you are. I wore a big red patch on my back, and was very glad I did. In the modern attack there is bound to be a tremendous mixing up of units and it is an advantage for people to know who is talking to them. There is no doubt of the enormous value of discipline; the power to make people do things against their will or inclination: an absolute fear to disobey or not to comply strictly with an order. Co-operation between units is very essential. The seeking of cover can be overdone. Throughout these four days no man ever disobeyed or showed any inclination to disobey any order I gave, and it was a mighty strong position they had to take. All honour to the living, still more honour to the dead.

The hospital arrangements were bad: landing on a strange country by surprise, I dare say more was not possible: men very badly wounded had to lie two days on the beach waiting a hospital ship: water was scarce; they were constantly being shelled. But the less said about what happened at Helles and at the landing as regards the wounded the better; I can never forget all I saw and all I thought. The Indian Brigade hospital arrangements were really jolly good, and Dallas, Cornish and I had much to be thankful for Captain Phipson our doctor, was splendid throughout; he helped everybody, British and Indian alike; an absolutely model regimental doctor, gallant and willing, and very good indeed at his job. He kept me going wonderfully.

And so ended the great battle for Chank Bair: we had held victory in our grasp, and had the whole operation been a success, nothing would have been too good for us; as it is we must suffer with the failure: it is galling to think of how many of one's battalion are no longer alive, through whose example and death we gained our objective, only to be given up because others could not reach us or support us. To one alive "a crowded hour of glorious life is better than an age without name"; but I had left the battlefield a changed man; all my ambitions to be a successful soldier have gone; knowing all I now know, I feel the responsibility, the murderous responsibility, that rests on the shoulders of an inefficient soldier or one who has passed his prime to command.

Chapter V
The Capture Of Hill 60

10th August – 14th September – I have not kept a diary through this period largely, I am afraid, through the fact that it has been all I can do to get through the day's work; for some period of this time my wound upset me considerably; something went wrong with the nerves of my leg, then followed a touch of dysentery, and subsequently low fever (making my back ache beyond words) troubled me for about a week. However, I was able to hang on, and am now, I trust, all right.

The position we are now in is a long line from Anzac to the hills above Suvla Bay, a line about 12 miles in length, varying from 500 to 1000 yards from the sea; The Turks overlook us from the hills 1000 feet above, and we are literally hanging on by our eyelids. A formidable, repeated and continues attack and we shall be in the sea.

As I have already explained my regiment succeeded in gaining and practically holding for 36 hours a portion of the Chanak Bair and Sari Bair ridges, which command the whole peninsula and very much poor us. What a difference to us all if we could have been supported. It was lack of co-operation and co-ordination; lack of those who control more than one regiment, i.e., generals and staff recognising that the actual presence of some staff officers was required, and that such a country and the immense difficulty of intercommunication verbal and personal orders were required. When the operations come to be criticised and examined it will be found how terribly the higher units, divisions and brigade, were split, and how impossible it was for battalion and other commanders to know what to do when many of them did not know whom they were really under.

Had my regiment been anywhere near its full strength in British Officers, the situation might still have been saved, as there might still have been someone left who could get down the hill and demand assistance. I was alone, crippled, and even had I been perfectly well I doubt if I would have been justified in leaving my battalion alone in a most critical point which might have been lost during my absence. On that ridge I watched the Turkish Reinforcements coming over from the Asia Minor side, and the opportunity of a lifetime and of victory slowly slipping from our grasp. A maddening sensation, so near and yet so far; what can one say of an organisation which sends a battalion into an attack on which Eastern Europe hung, which was being watched by the world, which had been prepared and planned for three months, with only 50 per cent of its officers? And had we been at full strength it might just have turned the scales. And yet on the line of communications between Alexandria and Anzac were at least 12 to 15 officers for the Indian Brigade, hung up and unable to get on. My regiment clung to its position on the ridge (or better say just below; it would have been madness t remain just on top, where artillery fire could easily dislodge us) all the 9th, the night of the 9th–10th, and up to 11am on the 10th, when messages were received from the British regiments close to us that they had received orders to retire, and had already done so! We were left "en l'air" and felt it. Half an hour later orders were received for us to come down the hill and join Brigade Headquarters 1000 feet below. It was a sad moment; victory had slipped us, and I feel absolutely certain that the Gallipoli peninsula and the Straits will never be ours. Captain Tomes had taken command for the retirement, but was killed within ten minutes of dawn; another great loss to his regiment, our regiment, and to his country, a splendid officer of the very best type, a high ideal of his duty, and capacity and courage to see that ideal through.

The retirement was carried out most successfully: all the stores and wounded were brought down (except the telephone wires): it was impossible to carry down all the rifles of the dead and wounded, and so all their bolts were removed, and they were left behind; not a man broke from the walk, and the operation was carried out wonderfully well. The men were utterly worn out, suffering from want of sleep, hunger and thirst, and the value of discipline and peace training were strongly exemplified. The Subedar Major Gumba Sing Pun and Captain Phipson our doctor, were splendid.

The evening saw us 1000 feet below, back within half a mile of the sea, where utterly worn out as we were, we had to dig ourselves in the continuous line it had now been decided to hold. The regiment had lost very heavily indeed: all its British officers except one wounded had gone, 60 per cent of the Gurkha officers and 52 per cent of the rank and file. Very little will be heard, probably of this operation, as the combined operation was a failure, but the feat of the 6th Gurkhas is a great one, and considered a great one by everybody in the battle. I must not labour the opportunity lost too much; to me it is a bitter disappointment, and perhaps I, more than anyone else, know how very close a thing it was, and how little things may in a war may turn the scale; generally it was a lack of appreciation of the tactical situation and want of recognition that the difference between victory and defeat meant a vast difference, morally and politically to our cause. Most of the telephone wires of all units were cut during the operations. I wonder how many C.O.s kept those below informed at frequent intervals how matters stood. The fact that five battalions under General Baldwin were to have joined me on the morning of the 9th at 5.15am, and lost their way was only one of the very unfortunate errors which stopped us shortening this campaign and probably the whole war by months.

Lieutenant Bear, Indian Army Reserve, who had sprained his ankle on the 4th, rejoined on the 10th. Captain Lloyd, 5th Gurkhas, took over command of the regiment on the 12th during my absence in hospital, but was killed on the 14th when showing the G.O.C Brigade over the new line we had taken up. Captain J.O. Airy (retired Indian Army) Lieut. Fashen, 9th Bhopals, Lieut. Leman, 30th Punjabis joined on this day: all these officers came from England, and if any energy had been shown on the lines of communications, could have joined before the great advance, when their services would have been invaluable. Captain Airy has been serving with eth 12th Essex in England, Lieut. Fashen has been in France with the 9thBhopals and Lieut. Leman with the 2nd Gurkhas in the same place, where he was badly wounded.

I rejoined on the 16th, as the G.O.C. informed me there was to be another advance on the 21st, and it was essential to get back. I was still in a good deal of pain, but the excitement, unhealthy as it was, of the next few days did wonders to my leg, and seemed to pull all the nerves and tissues back into their proper place.

The whole of the period from now up to the 21st was spent in consolidating our position. It was heavy work, as we could only work by night, and to sleep by day with sun and flies is a nearly impossible feat. We were all pretty well worn out in the previous battle. The anxiety and strain on British officers is very great, as the most careful watch has to be kept, and the whole firing line must be ready at a moment's notice.

Whilst we were busy between 6th and 10th August, the 9th Corps had been disembarked at Suvla Bay, and should have advanced and held Chanak Bair ridge on our left with their right, and their left well forward covering Suvla bay. One is given no information of what is happening around one, but one can easily gather that this plan has been a colossal failure, accompanied by tremendous losses. It is for this reason that we have for the present taken up a defensive position.

21st August – At 9am orders were issues to the Brigade to make an advance of 1000 yards and entrench in a new position at the end of it: our left flank was to rest on an important well called Susuk Kuyu and our right on a hill height 60 feet (Hill 60): the latter was covered with low scrub and jungle, and a formidable looking position. Besides the Indian Brigade, the Connaught Rangers and the 18th Australian regiment were to advance as well. It is immensely trying to work these advances in the open in the face of modern weapons, and must be done fast, as once men get down for any period human endurance makes it almost impossible for them to get up again.

I had to go and see the G.O.C. (Cox) at 10am and the conference was over at 11: the advance was to be at 4pm, and there was little time to cook two days rations, pack up all our kit, and give all the orders and instructions necessary before such a manoeuvre. At Midday, from our line of trenches, I showed all our officers and N.C.O.s the exact line the battalion was to advance, and impressed on all the great advantage of getting over the ground fast and together, so that the enemy should not be able to concentrate their fire on a few. There was to be an hour's preliminary bombardment of the enemy trenches before we started. I watched the bombardment with dismay: it was poor in quantity and quality, and when an order reached me that the advance was to be at 4.30pm and not 4 I felt again that a feeling of doubt was in the air. Considering that there was a good moon I shall never understand why this advance could not have been done by night, say for 600 yards and then we could have dug ourselves in: after consolidating that position we could have again moved forward. This would have been infinitely less costly, and I am firmly of belief every bit as successful as our deadly advance was.

The moment for the 5th and 10th Gurkhas to advance was approaching, whilst I was to follow in support, the 14th Sikhs were to remain in their trenches and give covering fire: quite a pleasant occupation. All our regiments had hardly yet got over the shock of fighting between the 6th and 10th, and every face was strained and drawn. One does not like to say good-bye and good luck as each double company goes off: it gives away what is one's heart, but one knows that the next roll-call must be a sad affair

The moment came, the artillery bombardment ceased Why? The enemy's trenches were 1000 yards off, why not have continued it till we got within 200 yards. I watched the 5th start: a deadly operation getting out of safe trenches and taking to the open: the moment they rose a fusillade of musketry, shrapnel and maxim was round us all. It made them think, and the advance commenced slowly, but surely it went on. In the first 100 yards I saw four out of their seven British officers go down; I was ordered to reinforce both the 5th and 10th, and moved up three double companies to do so. Two out of my five British officers were hit, Lieut. Greene, most gallantly leading his double company which had only joined three days before, killed by a shell, and Lieut. Leman wounded: he bravely hung on until our objective was gained: the Subedar Major Gamba Sing Pun is wounded in the head with a shrapnel quite close to me: a truly magnificent man, most gallant and fearless, with no thought for anything but the name of the Gurkha and his regiment. When he fell he told his orderly to fetch me; he was nearly senseless; he said "Sahib, what will you do without me? What will the regiment do? I do not mind death – what is that! But you want me and the regiment wants me, and I cannot be spared." He took my hand, and the tears poured from his eyes. I told him to be of good cheer, and said we would all carry on to the end. He would not be comforted, but I had to leave him to be carried back by the stretcher-bearers, as the last double company with which I was had to go on.

I shall never forget that scene: surely no soldier's farewell has ever been under more thrilling circumstances: a rain of iron, a roar which made it difficult to hear, death and dying and suffering, gallantry and courage all around. War is horrible and loathsome, but it is redeemed by scenes such as these, which show what education can do towards making one's life a willing sacrifice. Lieut. Hay-Webb was close to me, shot through the stomach and looking very grey; one knew his chance of recovery were small, and such they proved to be, as in 36 hours he had done all a soldier can do and given up his life. Lieut. Greene, attached to us and Lieut. Comyns (5th Gurkhas) I found close together and buried them at dawn behind a slight rise where we were hidden from view. A very shallow grave, time was precious; a little more light and we would be seen. Both were very stiff, and not easy to manipulate: at the graveside were Airy, Phipson and myself, and two or three Gurkhas. A soldier's funeral with a vengeance: I want no more of the glories of war. My heart went out to the two afflicted families whom I was representing in the gleam of dawn on August 22nd: it was a risky funeral; the comfort that it was done, to their families, and the deep respect one owed them, is one's reward.

Dawn of the 22nd saw the left of our line on their objective, the right 200 yards short of Hill 60, and a wide gap in the middle held by myself and a double company just scratched into the ground. No movement through the day was possible, but at dusk orders reached me to join up the 10th and 5th and dig myself in between them. Some of my battalion were with the 5th, some with the 10th, and as these regiments were digging in for their lives I did not like to withdraw any of my men from them. With what I had I laid out a line connecting these two regiments and commenced to get down. It is creepy work, this digging a line of trenches in absolutely open country in full moonlight with the enemy about 250 yards away and 60 feet above one. A very heavy fire opened on me just as we started work, and before we could throw ourselves on the ground five men had been hit. By the morning we had dug ourselves some form of shelter and had roughly joined the two regiments together. We still had no communication with the rear and our food had to be brought up at night. One gets two meals a day, one at 4.30 a.m., just before dawn, another at 7.30 p.m., after dusk, and nothing in between. The heat by day is very great and trying; there is no shelter from it, and the flies are maddening.

August 23rd – Another advance to get the remainder of Hill 60, in which my battalion had to co-operate by gaining another 100 yards. After a tremendous bombardment the forward move was made, but the casualties were appalling. The objective is gained and so after three days fighting we find ourselves at last in touch with eth 9th Corps, who have joined up with us at Susuk Kuyu; it was with great relief we suddenly found the Warwickshire Yeomanry on our left. Before this advance there was a big gap between ourselves (the Australian and New Zealand Army Corps) and the 9th Corps. This gap is filled by throwing in between us a large force of Yeomanry from Egypt, advancing the right flank of the 9th Corps and the left flank (which was our brigade) of our Corps. Of the 4,000 employed in our brigade for this manoeuvre 2,000 were killed and wounded, the only Australian regiment employed losing nearly 800. The whole place is strewn with bodies Gurkhas, Australians, Connaught Ranger; the smell, another of the minor horrors of war, is appalling, the sights revolting and disgusting. Our work is so heavy that we cannot ad to it by burying the bodies. During the digging of our fresh line on the 23rd, to consolidate the position won, we hear in front of us groaning, and creeping up found two wounded Connaught Rangers who have been lying out unable to move since the afternoon of the 21st, and who were nearing starvation. Their condition, having been unable to move, was very horrible. Considering the medical people knew exactly over what country the advance had been made and that we had two nights in succession been digging in the open one would have thought the ground might have been thoroughly searched for wounded people.

By the 25th we have dug ourselves in, and the work is not quite so heavy, but it is a most trying existence living underground, unable to show one's head and maddened by flies. The food difficulty, too is serious; it is cooked two miles behind, and by the time it has reached us and been thoroughly messed about by orderlies, it is almost uneatable, especially at 4.30 a.m. in the morning. One feels oneself daily getting weaker, and trench fever and back aches trouble one. I have sent to India for immediate despatch for one big and eight small tiffin carriers, in which food can be placed and kept hot whilst it is brought up to the trenches. The British officer is a most valuable person; he is irreplaceable, and the supply is getting exhausted. Most of them are so anxiously looking after their men that they neglect their own personal welfare and comfort with very bad results. We have had one or two cases of sickness from nothing else. I have now only Airy, Fasken, Bear and myself left. The middle two will soon go sick; they are looking wretchedly weak and ill. There has been lack of forethought with the mess, and we are out of all stores. One would give one's soul for a little porridge for breakfast, a little cake for tea.

27th August – we have been busy consolidating our position and getting communication with the rear by long and deep communications trenches. Captain Molloy, commanding 5th Gurkhas, has been hit, and I have temporarily to command both regiments, and move up to Hill 60, very close to the Turks, an important and tactical feature, and a dangerous and anxious position, distinctly worse than the one we occupy. Fortunately Captain Ryan has rejoined, an invaluable asset to the regiment, and I leave him in practical command of the 6th. 2nd Lieut. Bear, as I anticipated, has been compelled to go sick. There are still heaps and heaps of corpses about, and the smell is the most appalling thing of its nature one can imagine. All the officers the 5th possess are four officers of the Indian Army Reserve, one of whom is really rather good indeed.

The whole of the time from now on to the 10th September is spent by both the 5th and 6th in consolidating their positions. We have regularly four or five casualties a day, and only about 200 men left in each battalion. We push out patrols regularly every night to let the Turks know we are not asleep. It requires a gallant man to creep up towards the enemy's trenches only a hundred and odd yards away, knowing that any moment may be his last. I hope we may not be yet for another advance; it will be difficult to get out of this shattered unit, and the loss in British officers will be truly great.

The 4th Gurkhas, 1000 strong, under Lieut-Colonel Bateman-Champain, an old friend of mine, and a fine soldier are expected to reach here about 10th September, and their arrival will be a godsend. We have not had a day or night off, and constant fighting since August 6th. On the 14th September we move out of the firing line into reserve, about 600 yards behind. We are just as likely to be shelled, but at any rate we get our nights in bed. If anyone wants to know what exhaustion is, let them command or be with an Indian regiment in any capacity in constant touch with an active European enemy for 40 days without rest. It has to be gone through to be believed. The staff do not understand it, because they have not done it, and are, as a whole, nothing like considerate enough to those who do. One has to spend a good deal of time impressing on them what it means, not for one's own sake, but for those for whose lives one is responsible, who have served one so splendidly, so willingly, and so well. I dare say it makes one unpopular, but as I want nothing I do not care. If there is anything of real importance or urgency one is ready to do anything, but what one dislikes is being got at to do all sorts of things that are quiet irrelevant and which probably the General does not even know the Staff is doing.

An excellent officer called Captain Gout 94th Russell's Infantry, has been sent to us. He has been with Gurkhas for the past six months or so in France, and has been wounded three times. He is very enthusiastic about the work done by the Gurkhas in France. This somewhat relives the strain, but I still have not got even four double company commanders and an adjutant, to say nothing of all the important official, a quartermaster, a machine gun officer, or a signalling officer.

Generally, it would look now as if things were at a standstill and deadlock. It will cost us thousands if we are to break through the Turkish trenches which now envelope us, and it will cost them more considerably, I trust, if they try to break through us.

Winter is approaching; the weather at night is getting very cold; we hear no breath of fitting us out for the winter, and we shall have terrible sickness if they do not.

I have no idea what the future holds forth, what our subsequent movements may be. I can only speak of the narrow front we hold and one knows little of what goes on elsewhere. We have had our chance here, and we have missed it. Towering above us is Sari Bair ridge, on which we should be safely ensconced and are not, and had we held it Achi Baba and Krithia must have fallen. I never look up to those rugged heights without a sigh of bitter regret; on the topmost summit lie the graves of immortal memory, Tomes and le Marchand, the highest point ever held by any of the force, and all up those slopes lie bodies of our men who died to enable some of us to get to the top; all unburied and uncared for, and among them poor Underhill, who is missing, and certainly there.

Throughout this period my guardian angel was in the air, as I escaped unwounded and untouched. In any advance everyone has narrow escapes, and one expected every minute to go down. On September 5th I had a most exceptionally close shave: a shrapnel burst not far away from me, and suddenly I felt a blow on my right shoulder and heard a noise behind; the empty case of an exploded 10pr shrapnel had carried off my shoulder strap and dropped just behind me. It had travelled so fast that I did not even see it, and had it caught my shoulder or head I must have been killed.

Such are the fortunes of war. One man is killed, another is not, and it is beyond my capacity to say how the selection is made.

Chapter VI
Holding The Line

14th September – 4th October – On September 14th we were withdrawn into support about 500 yards from the firing line. This means freedom from rifle fire, an immense relief from responsibility, but, of course as much liability to be shelled at any hour as before, restricting one's movements entirely to the trenches. Yesterday for instance, September 30th, we were the centre of a high explosives bombardment; the ranging was accurate, and we should have suffered very heavily except for the fortunate occurrence that few of them burst. How one loathes the sound of high explosive humming towards one; if it lands near you you are done; you cannot evade it like you can shrapnel; it tears through everything and the wounds from it are too horrible for words. Bombs are bad enough, but there is not that awful sound of them coming nearer and nearer. I hate to pass down our lines after a bombardment; all the faces are white and scared; no living man could feel anything but pity for what their faces portray; the Gurkha is a brave and plucky little chap, but it is devilish hard to keep up a smile with high explosives flying round. These are times one rather feels sad for the Indian Soldier; he has no idea what he is fighting; he is doing what he is told for the sake of the British officer he loves, and he is fighting a very different war to what he has been taught or for what he has been organised. If ever regiments want 30 officers we do, and I would add 30 British N.C.O.s, they would make up the initiative and resource required in modern war, and which the Indian generally has not got. Some unquestionably have it, but the men will not follow them or do anything for them like they will for us.

Life is of course, extremely dull; movement slow and very

limited in direction, as one is not supposed to wander into trenches of other units or brigade. The actual brain work is nil. However, the freedom from anxiety and the rest to one's nerves are such that even living an underground existence as one does one is contented and happy. But our position tactically is appalling; if the Turks can get plenty of artillery and ammunition they must be able to make our position untenable. They have unlimited men, and any amount, I believe of civil labour; they can get their troops well out of range of all our guns when it comes to their time to give them a rest, and they have spent the past month in absolutely investing us. To break out will be a most costly business indeed, especially as they must see our reinforcements coming by sea, and be able to gather approximately when the day approaches. We are in a country without a road or railway, and transport and all intercommunication is slow and difficult. As we take up a wider area we require more troops to hold it. In fact, we have taken on a vast campaign in itself as a secondary effort.

We have had some very cold blasts of weather, and when the northerly wind gets up it is a most biting one, and simply even now seems to penetrate everything. What one really looks forward to is one's mail and daily papers. To a battalion commander in this kind of life there is not much chance of being able to fill up his day; he cannot make out or think of plans for the future, as he knows nothing, and one rather envies those who do, and those in whose hand the "bundobust" of the campaign lies. We can hold no parades, as every man must keep below the level of the earth or will draw fire; by night we undertake two or three hours digging to give the men exercise, and to carry out general improvements to our position. Our fellows are superb diggers.

I cannot give away anything in the diary, but there are tactical errors being made which amaze me. That they are errors would seem to me undoubted, and they were the first thing that attracted the attention of the officers of the 4th Gurkhas who have just reached here from France.

We have one or two occasions sent large digging parties up to the firing line at night, as in parts it has been decided to push our line up a bit nearer the Turks. It is feared if we do not do this they may. We have never had any rain since I joined, but I fancy that it may be expected any day now, and what the effect will be it will be interesting to see. We might find the whole of the ground we are in in a swamp, and the trenches liable to fall in, which would be the very devil. I fancy when the winter comes on we shall find it very cold, and God knows we have enough to put up with now.

The regiment has now been brought up practically to full strength as regards men. This has been done by a draft of about 300 from Abbottabad, chiefly little recruit boys of only seven months service, and 100 men of ours whom we had sent earlier in the war as a reinforcement to the 4th Gurkhas from Abbottabad. It seems only right that they should on their arrival here give them back to us. They are all looking splendidly fit, and have evidently been well fed, housed and looked after; they also seem to have come full of spirit. A good many drafts of returned wounded men have been coming in, though it is difficult to imagine that these all retain their original keenness, and one feels a sincere sympathy with them, which one does not show, but only congratulates them on their spirit in coming back. As regards British officers, I have still only half my number, and it makes it most difficult to carry on efficiently. Lieut. Fasken, as I had already anticipated, has gone sick, also Lieut. Bear, and 2nd Lieut. Hearsay, both of the Indian Army Reserve, and originally rankers in the Ceylon Planters' Corps. Captain Gout, who has been wounded three times in France when attached to Gurkha regiments, has come to try his luck in the Dardanelles and strikes me as a particularly good, keen and able officer.

Captain Bagot Harte, 2/6th Gurkhas and 2ndlieut. Hart, I.A.R. (he was in the Bank of Bengal, Calcutta) joined with the new draft.

I have therefore now: Self, C.O., Capt. Gout, second in command and Double Company Commander, Captain Bagot Harte, D.C. Commander; Captain Airy, D.C. Commander; Captain Ryan, Adjutant; 2ndlieut. Hart, D.C. Commander. Instead of twelve officers; all the officers required for the expert services are non-available, and if any officer now goes sick I have not an officer for a double company. It means a tremendous lot of work for the British officers when we are in the firing line, and one does want them very badly when important patrols go out, but at present I cannot place any of them on hazardous work, which they do not, fine fellows that they are, at all appreciate. If anything happened to any of them it would be immensely difficult to carry on efficiently.

We have just hears that the "Ramzan" carrying drafts for the Indian Brigade, has been torpedoed, but we do not know yet whether any of the British officers who must have been on board have been saved. Rumour also says that some of our winter clothing is on board, and if that has gone to the bottom there are some very evil days ahead.

The men are now very good; they never grumble, though many of them have been away from their homes for a year, and they keep cheery under none too pleasant surroundings. It is impossible to expect them to have quite the same enthusiasm about the war that we have. The British troops do not look well as a whole and stomach troubles have played the very devil with them. I watch those with whom I have to work sticking it out, but getting weaker and weaker every day.

Sir Ian Hamilton visited our lines the other day. It struck me as rather strange that he should not have had one word to say to any officer about how well we had done, especially between 6th and 10th August. That the regiment did do remarkably well is admitted throughout the peninsula. However, in a big army a battalion is only a very small pawn; it must be content with the self-consciousness that it has done its duty.

On October 4th we go back into the firing line, and are detailed for the protection of Hill 60, an important tactical feature, where every night there is much bombing and "strafing".

A dull uninteresting diary, but the strength of our troops here I cannot put in, nor anything that would give anything away which at present juncture considerably restricts my pen. We have suffered no officer casualties, and only a few men since I last wrote, because in reserve we remain glued to our trenches and dug-outs.

Shortly after writing this a heavy high explosive bombardment commenced on a small machine gun range we had put up, with the result that we lost 25 per cent of our machine gunners. Again if their shell had been really effective, we should have lost many more. Undoubtedly the range was taken for a gun emplacement. It tends to show that the Turks have plenty of shell when they get a target they wish to obliterate. It also indicates that they dread our heavy artillery more than anything else. From the heights above it is plain they can not only see our every action, but can bombard us wherever and whenever they wish, in the firing line, in support and in reserve. All one can reiterate is, thank God, they seem short of ammunition, as they certainly are sparing in its use.

And now as regards the much discussed question of the staff. In this kind of warfare – modern, presumably – one is quite as a regimental officer divorced from the staff, infinitely more so than in peace. Visiting trenches is a very slow and tiring business, and they have naturally much work of their own, and cannot afford to come round and check people; also it is a dangerous thing coming round the firing line, and not over convenient to tired troops who are trying to get by day what they get little of by night, some sleep. Your Brigade Major and Staff Captain you see but I have never spoken to another Staff Officer on this peninsula and practically never seen one. Great stress is laid in peace time that touch should be kept in peace between staff and units; it certainly is not in this war, as far as I have seen. There can be no question that the best brains, the best thinkers, and best soldiers, and the most energetic, are wanted as G.O.C.s particularly, and then their staff. They control everything, and it is only by the closest co-operation, by exceptionally good forethought and staff work, that heavy casualties can be avoided. In this force we have mighty few regular officers. The class of regular officer as a whole in this brigade I consider stands out, and I would even be inclined to go as far as saying that most of them would be better employed elsewhere, and that the loss of the men who could not remain without officers would be made up for by the experience these officers could bring to beat. I only watch the local gazette and know how few regular officers now exist in this force, and how many really important staff appointments are now held by armatures. I should be interested to see the method of selection; it is not a difficult one to guess. Our R.E., our Ordnance, our A.S.C., are all , or nearly all, Territorials or New Army, with very little training, comparatively speaking, and the staff of the division to which I belong has not any too highly qualified officers upon it. But it must be remembered I speak only as a battalion commander with limited range, but if with that limited range one can observe a good deal, how much more might one observe if opportunity allowed that view to be widened?

Under the conditions in which we live it would seem impractical that any regiment can keep up its dash; as I have already said we never move from trenches, we cannot. In France they do a week or ten Days in and a week or ten days out. During the latter they route march and make up for the sedentary and almost impossible existence of trench life utterly unrelieved. This regiment would, I am sure have the greatest difficulty in marching 15 miles. Fortunately, indeed we come from a month's rest at Imbros to the biggest fight that one could ever wish to be in from the 6th to 10th August, and during that month we had, after the first week, route marched, night marched, dug, run all over the hills, and left for Anzac thoroughly fit. We started 12 officers and 750 men. This battalion has now lost in casualties 22 officers and nearly 800 men, and is, of course are an entirely different unit to what it started. A modern war of any length is a war of inefficiency: casualties and destruction smash up your machinery, and you have to carry on with substitutes who are less and efficient. Fortunately it is the same on both sides, and it is the least inefficient who becomes the victor. The one who stops up the leaking holes best, the one who keeps up hope, and though recognising all the inefficiency with despair, remembers that it is probably – nay, let us say certainly – worse across the hundred yards of hill and plain that separate us from an enemy who at any rate is brave, and has, as far as we know, always played the game. If we were to be given tomorrow a month's rest at Imbros it would be a month of genuine hard work; It would be a month of trying to make 800 men without genuine cohesion into a trained battalion.

The Australians and new Zealanders are very fine troops, full of dash, fine stamina, and had they only discipline and did not despise that absolute essential of modern war – in fact, of all war – I can picture no finer troops in the world. Their enormous advantage is they do not want leading, and they do not want example, that costly work which deprives you of your best men at the time that they are most wanted, every man individually does his job, gets ahead and wants no call to do so. With all our troops it is different, and those who can lead and are brave enough to do so are, alas the first to fall so often, and so difficult to replace. The New Army has been, I express an opinion only, but one, I think, which is generally felt here, a little disappointing. Of course, the work that it has been asked to carry out has been a stupendously high trial, and would to have been done efficiently and well, have required our very best regular troops. Sickness has in addition played the very devil with them, and failure, ever, so far to obtain their objectives. They lack somewhat in dash because they want leading, and would assuredly follow leaders, but these seem lacking. A leader is either born or made. If he is born he is very soon, of whatever training, a remarkably fine officer; but if he has to be made he cannot be produced in a few months; it is an experience of years. Despite the very little training of the Australian and New Zealander, I believe if any officer on this peninsula was given a regiment for a job he would choose an Australian regiment first before any of our New Army.

The Indian Brigade has no white troops in it, and it has done splendidly. Nobody on this peninsula who has been with them can combat that; its discipline, cleanliness, health and spirit are very good. But to have an Indian unit at its very best, where material is good, they should have 30 officers, the same as every other regiment in our Army, and I would add 30 N.C.O.s. A white man is required with patrols because in modern war he can be relied upon to report what he has seen; he would presumably be a picked man, and he would not be taken in by the wiles of the enemy. We cannot afford to send out officers, not even if we had 30, and should have N.C.O.s

Small fatigue parties doing work which is utterly novel to them in a strange country want an N.C.O. with them who can talk English; for every little thing we have to send a British officer, which is wrong, and wears them out over little matters of administration. Unless we do this a reputation cannot be maintained. With 30 British officers and 30

N.C.O.s these regiments would also be second to none in the world. They are hardy, live on little, have very strong guts, are absolutely willing and anxious to please, and have tons of spirit, and do not fear death. Under the strange conditions the average Indian officer is a "wash out." In peace he does a lot of work; in war you have to do it all his as well as yours own. The whole thing is beyond him. He is not young, and the novelty upsets his equilibrium, which with few exceptions, he never regains. He can very rarely meet a change of conditions in an emergency.

Modern war is won by forethought, machinery, minute co-operation between artillery and infantry, good staff work, and the individual work of each soldier when the machine moves to the attack or is fighting in defence. There are only three or four men between each traverse to a trench. Movement along a trench is most difficult, as the wider the trench the greater space there is for the enemy's high explosive to catch you. It is that, and the bomb, which are our most dreaded enemies. There can therefore be little leadership in the defence, and in the attack leaders fall quick, and it is only where all are doing alike and no picked target presents itself that the enemy's musketry begins to get wild and comparatively ineffective

Chapter VII
Another Advance

15th September – December 3rd – I closed my last diary on or about 15th September, and from that date till October 4th we remained in a reserve line about 500 to 600 yards behind the firing line. During all this period of rest the men did about four hours digging at night at different portions of the Brigade area, more communications trenches, and deepening those already in use. I would have liked to have seen a good deal of this time spent in making an impregnable position behind, or as far impregnable as possible, considering the great disadvantage of the tactical positions we hold compared with the enemy.

On October 4th we again went up to the firing line, our right resting on the important – or made important – tactical feature of Hill 60, the top 15 yards of which are still in the position of the Turks, and which despite all the great struggling of the 21st to 24th August, we did not succeed in wrestling from them. At this point our trenches are under 20 yards apart. We placed four companies in the firing line and four companies in support along a front of 250 yards.

Orders had been issued for the whole Indian Brigade to advance about 150 yards to straighten out our line which was below. The advance on the extreme right and left was only a short distance, as is clear from the sketch

Susuk-Kuyu Well ɣ------- -- --------- -- -------- -- --------|-- ----------ɣ Hill 60

```
....                                           ....
....                                           ....
      .................................................
```

....	Our Trenches
------------	New proposed line
———————	Turkish trenches

Patrols were pushed out the night before this work was undertaken, with a view to discovering whether we were likely to find bodies of Turks in the open who might find we had advanced our lines before we could dig down sufficiently low to give cover. We marked out these lines of trenches by a new method, using empty sandbags in this fashion.

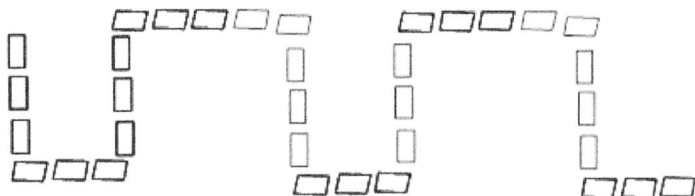

This was done by an officer and four men, two of them carrying the empty sandbags; it proved a most rapid and efficacious way of working. Pacing and measuring are done away with as the number of sandbags necessary to give the width of a bay and the size of a traverse is carefully fixed beforehand. When the battalion move up to the line it cannot miss it, and can commence work at once. As soon as each man has picked out the line from the sandbags he has to work on, he can fill the empty sandbags in front of him immediately, and thus gain very rapidly a little cover. A curious episode occurred shortly after the brigade had taken up the line and work had commenced. There were in front 28 men as a covering party told off from one regiment, and as far as could be discovered some of these men came back on to the diggers and reported the Turks were advancing. A few men got panic struck, and ran back into the trenches we had just quitted; the fever spread, and in a few minute there was nobody on the whole line but a few officers and men who stood their ground. This rapid retirement created a considerable amount of noise, and it was decided to keep the men back in their old line until their sangfroid had returned. A large proportion of the covering party had remained out, and there was not a sign of a Turk. It is significant how a few men lacking in courage can produce a disaster, as this might well have been. Had the Turks been advancing nothing could have been more disconcerting to them than to come suddenly under heavy fire from us 150 yards before they expected. From one's experience of night work the result would almost certainly have been that they would have very rapidly returned whence they came. Within an hour the whole brigade was back on the line, working quietly and happily, and by dawn had got themselves sufficiently down to ensure cover. It was however considered advisable not to occupy these trenches during the next day. The communications trenches to the rear had not been completed, and if the new work was bombarded the men would suffer heavily and be unable to evacuate them temporarily. The only fear was that the Turks might try and seize them before we got up to them that night, but such an eventuality was not a difficult one to deal with if one was prepared for it. The work was completed successfully during the next night, and the trenches were fit for occupation and retention by dawn, and it was decided to hold them. The bit on our extreme right, which was as I have already said, very close to the Turks, had to be done entirely by sapping, and we took a considerable time longer there to complete the line.

On October 9th Captain Gout reported the use of gas by the enemy opposite him, and respirators were immediately put on. There seems however, some doubt now as to whether this report was correct, and if it was not only fumes of some distant bomb that made all the men's eyes smart so.

On October 10th we were bombed for the first time by good high explosives, really powerful stuff, which the Turks had not used before in this area. This points to a new supply of ammunition now being available.

A very decided drop in temperature took place on October 13th, and the North wind, when it gets up, is most bitterly cold and piercing.

During this period in the front line trenches the enemy used frequently to be heard digging on our front, and on every occasion when it was pronounced we fixed a time at which the whole battalion should fire three rounds rapid, and got artillery co-operating with us to fire a salvo on their trenches immediately on our opening fire. The idea was that the moment our fire broke out, the enemy would make for his trenches, and be caught just getting into them by shrapnel. It certainly had the effect of stopping the digging for some hours.

It is not possible at any time to show a head above the ground as the enemy's rifle fire is very accurate, and bunches of men invariably attract it.

After a fortnight of this work we were relieved and went back to support, where we had a great deal of fatigue duty to do almost entirely, of course, at night. In fact, in trench war it is in the day that is the time of peace, and the night the worry and anxiety.

On October 21st the weather became both wet and cold, and as we have no shelter beyond that provided by waterproof sheets the discomfort, amounting to genuine pain, that rain and cold must inflict is great. I wonder how one is to stick it out through the coming winter. I frankly dread it all, and cannot but see the clouds of disaster gathering ahead.

On October 28th a South-West gale got up causing a great rise in temperature (and return of the truly damnable fly), and up to 10th November the weather remained agreeably pleasant. On October 29th the enemy opened a severe but short bombardment of our whole position from Suvla bay to Anzac bases, the firing line and supports; they have evidently got more ammunition and better – a very disquieting thought.

On October 30th a draft of three British officers and 20 men joined us. This brings our strength up to 600 men and eight British officers, the largest number of the latter we have had since May 22nd. The new officers are captain Watson Smyth, 1st Brahmans, who was private secretary to Sir James Meston, Lieut-Governor of the United Provinces; Lieut. King-Salter of my own battalion, whom I last met at his father's funeral (he was commanding the Rifle Brigade) at Calcutta, and a young Calcutta merchant, by the name of Snodgrass, from Messrs. Pigott, Chapman & Co.

On November 3rd we were again ordered back to the firing line, and have been told to push our trenches up to within 25 to 40 yards of the Turks on the right of our line. This places us within bombing range, and will have to be done entirely by sapping: the ground is very hard and rocky, and as the distance to be completed is almost 120 yards, it will take us 20 days to complete, and it will be dangerous work throughout. We cannot sap more than two feet an hour at the very outside. Certain preliminaries have had to be undertaken, such as the selection of the alignment, points to commence, etc, and the work commences on November 7th.

I will take November 8th as a typical day of our life. We have not had one days rest or been out of fire since August 4th, and the strain is telling on everyone. The day is fairly quiet except for a bombardment of Hill 60 by our own heavy guns with high explosive. As at this point our trenches are only 12 yards away we clear out all our front trenches before it commences. As each shell lands the whole earth shakes and we wonder what the feelings of our enemy must be; he has probably evacuated his front line, as he will have noticed that our barbed wire is intact, and our chances of coming forward are therefore slight.

Immediately night falls the sniping becomes pretty heavy on both sides, and bombs are constantly being thrown; it is a pretty steady roar; both sides seem to be afraid the other is going to advance. I know we have no intention of doing so, and are hanging on by our eyelids, and only hope that they have none either. I always think that an attack of 10,000 men all pressed will certainly get through us. Suddenly a bomb followed immediately by another, lands in the front trench and a man is hit in the eye. The British troops on our right (the 7th Essex) immediately fire off their trench mortar, the bomb falls short, and lays out four of our men. A regular bombing match commences, in reality more of a "funk" fire than anything else and so the game continues, and from Hill 60 daily and nightly our strength is slowly trickling away, killed, wounded and sick.

I still know nothing of the intended plans, and I would not ask anything; the regimental officer's duty is to obey, and the fewer people who know the plans of the great the better. One must continue this trying existence without change, relief or relaxation. I am sorry for the men, as I know that some of them feel they can never get away. No man has ever left us except killed, wounded or sick, and the number who originally started with us is truly small and dwindling daily. Of course, new men join, but they are lamentably wanting in training, and here we can undertake nothing. After weeks of this sort of life without even one hour's marching and advance would be difficult.

Alas! Captain Ryan has to go sick. He has worn himself out with anxiety, and will be a very severe loss to me. He is a fine soldier, a sound tactician, and a brave comrade. It will add greatly to my work, but that cannot be helped. The best soldiers really are the finest animals, people without nerves, without much feeling, and pretty callous to pain and suffering. On them, there are not many of that type, war falls, comparatively speaking, lightly: but on everyone else it is a persistent strain to put up with almost everything that is distasteful. Imagine in ordinary life what it would be to attend a funeral every day: and yet through months on end that falls to one's daily lot.

November 10th to 17th saw us again in the trenches, and much the same daily routine. We get very little water and not too much digestible food, but generally my battalion is better off than most of the others. I always spend a good deal of my time among the men in the firing line, talking to them and encouraging them. I love them and admire them. Never has a soldier been better or more truly served. All honour to them and despite all they have been through I have practically never heard a man utter one word of complaint. They go through it all stolidly, and sickness has hardly affected them. Thank God they are pretty callous to death, and certainly have plenty of courage. Within the last fortnight I have lost over 50 per cent of my machine gunners through high explosive bombardments, many of the men who had done me splendidly through the campaign. Evidently the Turks go to great pains to locate machine guns. Every one of them should have some arrangement to conceal the flash at night and a silencer. The latter are I believe, like many other dire necessities, to be issued shortly!

The 17th to the 24th November saw us again in reserve. On the 22nd I was going down to the Ordnance stores to press upon them again the grave urgency of our winter clothing, accompanied by Captain Watson Smyth, when suddenly near Anzac a shrapnel burst straight in front of us. It came against the wind and I knew immediately that some of us were for it. I felt a terrible blow on my right hand and looked down to find it cut open and streaming with blood; a bullet had gone through the hand; another bullet had gone through Captain Watson Smyth's coat pocket, two mules had been killed close by, and a Sikh and Australian wounded. A mixed bag for "Beachy Bill" and a proof of how damned unsafe this peninsula is everywhere. I went to the nearest dressing station, where I fainted whilst the wound was being dressed. They said I had better leave the peninsula, as there was a fear from the position of wound of lockjaw, and its getting septic, but I got permission to stay on a few days and have it daily watched. I am afraid it will take a month to heal, but except to write and dress it does not greatly incapacitate me.

Chapter VIII
The Blizzard

On November 24th we entered the firing line for what proved to be a very eventful period, and my last. The wind suddenly turned to the north, heavy rain set in, a very great drop in temperature took place, a heavy fall of snow followed, and the cold became intense and bitter. Our trenches were literally flooded, and we were cut off from all communication with headquarters. We were done if the Turk attacked us, and should have had to fight it out where we stood. Lower and lower went the temperature till we had 16 degrees of frost, and every bone in my body ached with cold, and my wound became most painful. Sleeping and living in miserable dug-outs under such circumstances has to be gone through to be appreciated and understood. Think what it was for the N.C.O.s and men in the open trenches. Truly one was learning the necessity of courage. I rarely got a smile out of myself, and as I could neither shave or wash one probably looked even more miserable than one felt. In the middle of this blizzard orders reached me to take over the whole of Hill 60, as the 54th Division were leaving the peninsula. I had never seen this line of trenches, which were a perfect maze owing to the explosion of constant mines on both sides. These created new craters and filled up old ones. Both sides were still busy mining and the line was something of this nature:-

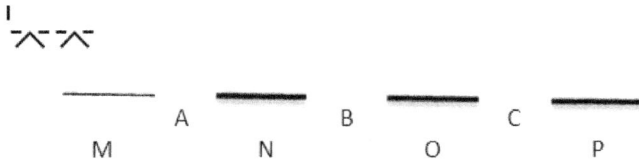

The positions marked A, B, and C, were cut underground to open out into spaces M, N, O, P, where a few rifles could stand. At M and P a trench had been dug, and bombing posts were made at the end. We were only 10 yards now from the Turks, and had great difficulty in even putting up a periscope. Bombs were flying about all day, and one always walked about with a blanket ready to throw it on a bomb if one came close to you and had not burst. I suppose through my life I have had most of the sensations which come from the life of an ordinary man, but since my arrival on this peninsula I have had a good many fresh ones, and most of them damned unpleasant. Here was a fresh one – the possibility of being blown into the air any moment when you were walking down the trenches by a mine, and at the same time to be n eth keenest look-out for a bomb.

The 54th Division having gone, we were now holding our line very weakly, and I was terribly anxious. The cold was terrible, and for the first time I was really abrupt to my superior officer, who telephoned up to me from a reasonably comfortable dug-out behind to know whether we could connect two trenches which were separated by a mine crater. I replied that we were doing all we could to live and we should be very lucky if we were able to do that, and could think of nothing else.

Fortunately the regiments with whom we are now working, the Welsh Horse, the Suffolk and Norfolk Yeomanry, are better than the east Anglian Division, who to me were very disappointing. I had a party of Welsh Horse to assist me in the bombing posts, and they are the best thing I have seen on the peninsula. I shall always remember with pride and admiration their splendid conduct throughout the blizzard, and their exceptional kindness and forethought to our men with whom they willing shared everything they had. In this maze of trenches if the Turks got into them it would be a single handed combat, and a few brave men are worth more than any number of others.

I have never seen, I doubt if I ever shall again such courage as I saw through this blizzard. Men found at the parapet facing the Turk with glassy eyes and stone dead, who gave up their lives rather than give in. Imagine the death of slow accepted torture. It is at such periods, and at such periods only, that one really does not seem afraid of death. It would be an honour to die in such a company and to be buried with them. Unfortunately we have suffered very heavily from frostbite. All the communication trenches have become knee and thigh deep in water, so that men and officers are constantly in freezing water, with no hope whatever of getting dry. We cannot allow them, so close to the Turks, to take off their boots, and unfortunately they have not been able to supply us with our winter stock of boots, two sizes too large, and a second pair of socks. Despite the intense pain the men have suffered, I never heard a complaint, and when I was able to I ordered all boots of men in support off, and asked the doctor to examine their feet. It was discovered that about 25 per cent of the whole regiment had frostbite, and were quite unable to carry on and off they had to go. This might have been prevented, and I frequently warned the ordnance and departments of the danger that was being run in not equipping men early with our full winter kit, and essentially gum boots or waders.

These rapid changes of line may be necessary, but they are dangerous, and one cannot help feeling that if the staff recognised a little more our difficulties we should get a little more notice of intended movements. A C.O. and his officers would then have ample time to reconnoitre the ground and get plans ready. Bad staff work between 25th November and 1st December cost the Indian Brigade 400 casualties.

On December 3rd my fighting career temporarily closed. I was standing just in the entrance to my dug-out, giving some notes to orderlies when there was a terrific roar; the world seemed to come on the top of me, and the next vivid memory I have was the communion on the hospital ship, "Gloucester Castle." An 8in. high explosive had come up against the wind and caught me standing up.

I cannot close this diary (written with the exception of the last few lines in a field service notebook on the peninsula) without expressing my intense admiration of the British officers who served with me. Throughout my time in command no officer game me a moment's trouble or caused me a moment's anxiety except as regards his safety. To all I owe a debt of gratitude I can never repay, to say nothing of those who had been responsible for the magnificent training of the machine that was placed in my hand. In particular I owe much to my two adjutants, Captain Ryan and Lieut. King-Salter. The latter was kindness and thoughtfulness itself to me through the blizzard, when I had damaged my hand. Captain Gout, Captain Watson Smyth and Captain Bagot Harte are all fine soldiers. And of what I have said of my brother countrymen I feel nearly every Gurkha officer and man. Properly led and given sufficient white men who possess the military training to give them confidence in positions of responsibility, they are an immense asset to an empire. I have seen hundreds die a hero's death. I have seen them had to hand with gigantic Turks, and I can never forget their glorious capture and retention of Hill 971, Sari Bair Ridge.

(I am glad to say that our medical officer, Captain Phipson, has since been awarded a D.S.O. and Captains Gout and Cornish the Military Cross. No one knows as well as I do how fully these decorations were deserved.

Appendix I

Ab   Headquarters

3338   New Zealand and Australian Divn.

                                         17.8.5

To Headquarters

         Australian and New Zealand Army Corps

         (Sir William Birdwood)

Attached copy of list of names recommended by Brig-General H.V. Cox, C.B., S.S.I, is forwarded for favorable commendation. I have the honour to submit the name of

Lieut. J.W.J. Le Marchand 1/6th G.R. This officer took part in the attack on Chanak Bair on 7th August, under major C.J.L. Allanson(recommended in my dispatch of 16th August for the reward of the V.C.) and was unfortunately killed on the top of the ridge. Brig-General Cox, in his first telegraphic report of the afternoon of the 9th August made use of the following expression

"I strongly recommend Major Allanson for the highest possible decoration for gallantry, and should have added the name of Lieut. Le Marchand had he lived."

Appendix II

EXTRACT FROM SIR IAN HAMILTON'S DESPATCH DATED 7TH JANUARY 1916

" At 4.30 am on August 9th the Chanak Bair Ridge and Hill Q were heavily shelled.

"General Baldwin's column (38th Infantry Brigade) had assembled in the Chailak Dere, and was moving up towards General Johnston's headquarters. Our plan contemplated the massing of this column immediately behind the trenches held by the New Zealand Infantry Brigade. There it was intended to launch the battalions in successive lines keeping them as much as possible on the high ground. Infinite trouble had been taken to ensure that the narrow track should be kept clear, guides also were provided; but in spite of all precautions the darkness, the rough scrub covered country, its sheer steepness, so delayed the column that they were unable to take full advantage of the configuration of the ground and, inclining to the left, did not reach the line of the Farm – Chanuk Bair till 5.15 a.m.

"In plain English Baldwin, owing to the darkness and the awful country, lost his way – through no fault of his own. The mischance was due to the fact that time did not admit of the careful reconnaissance of routes which is so essential where operations are to be carried out by night.

"And now under that fine leader, Major C.J.L. Allanson, the

6th Gurkhas of the 29th Indian Infantry Brigade, pressed up the slopes of Sari Bair crowned the heights of the col between Chanuk Bair and Hill Q, viewed far beneath them the waters of the Hellespont, viewed the Asiatic shores along which motor transport was bringing supplies to the lighters. Not only did the battalion, as well as some of the 6th South Lancashire Regiment. Reach the crest, but they began to attack down the far side of it, firing as they went at eth fast retreating enemy.

"But the fortune of war was against us. At this supreme moment Baldwin's column was still a long way from our trenches on the crest of Chanuk Bair, whence they should even now have been sweeping out towards Q along the whole ridge of the mountain. And instead of Baldwin's support came unexpectedly a salvo of heavy shell. These falling so suddenly among the stormers threw them into terrible confusion. The Turkish commander saw his chance; instantly his troops were rallied and brought back in a counter-charge, and the South Lancashires and Gurkhas, who had seen the promised land, and had seemed for a moment to have held victory in their grasp, were forced backwards over the crest and on to the lower slopes whence they had first started."

"But where was the main attack – where was Baldwin? When that bold but unlucky commander found he could not possibly reach our trenches on the top of Chanuk Bair in time to take effective part in the fight he deployed for attack where he stood, i.e. at the farm to the left of the New Zealand Brigade's trenches on Rhododendron Spur. Now his men were coming on in a fine style and, just as the Turks topped the ridge with shouts of elation, two companies of the 6th East Lancashire Regiment, together with the 10th Hampshire Regiment charged up our side of the slope with the bayonet.

"They had gained the high ground immediately below the

commanding knoll on Chanuk Bair, and a few minutes earlier would have joined hands with the Gurkhas and South Lancashires, and combined with them, would have carried all before them. But the Turks by this time were lining the whole of the high crest in overwhelming numbers. The New Army troops attacked with a fine audacity, but they were flung back from the height and then pressed still further down the slope, until General Baldwin had to with draw his command to the vicinity of the farm, whilst, the enemy, much encouraged, turned their attention to the new Zealand troops and the two New Army battalions of No. 1 Column still holding the south-west half of the main knoll of Chanuk Bair.

"Constant attacks, urged with fanatical persistence were met here with a sterner resolution, and although at the end of the day, our troops were greatly exhausted, they still kept their footing on the summit. And if that summit meant much to us, it meant even more to the Turks. For the ridge covered our landing places, it is true, but it covered not only the Turkish beaches at Kilia Leman and Maidos, but also the Narrows themselves and the roads leading northward to Bular and Constantinople.□

Appendix III

Gazette 5th November 2015

Distinguished Service Order

Major Cecil John Lyons Allanson, 1st Battalion 6th Gurkha Rifles

"For the most conspicuous gallantry and marked ability in leading his battalion to the attack on the Chanak Bair Ridge, Gallipoli Peninsula, Major Allanson with two companies succeeded in reaching the summit of the ridge under most destructive musketry fire from the enemy, where he was wounded by a bayonet thrust. When it was obvious that no support could reach him he skilfully withdrew his men, and notwithstanding the pain from his wound, remained with his battalion throughout the entire day, he being the only British Officer left.

Appendix IV

New Year's Honours 1st January 1916

COMMANDER OF THE MOST EMINENT ORDER OF THE INDIAN EMPIRE

Lieut.-Colonel C.J.L. Allanson D.S.O.1st Battalion 6th Gurkha Rifles

Printed in Great Britain
by Amazon